American Artist

Expressionism Photography

Copyright © 2018 by Dana Gregory

All rights reserved. No part of this book may be reproduced, scanned, or distributed in any printed or electronic form without permission

First Edition July 2018

Printed in the United States of America

ISBN-13: 978-1721756230
ISBN-10: 172175623X

Preface

"To me, photography is an art of observation. It's about finding something interesting in an ordinary place... I've found it has little to do with the things you see and everything to do with the way you see them." — Elliott Erwitt

The satisfaction of examining the heart of an artist is through a different optical lens than your own and seeing each picture open a whole new perspective with just how the camera is positioned for the shot. One comes to wonder what the original thoughts went into taking this picture and why there is a firm attention span in discovering the new versus the old. The beauty of this discovery is in the light touches with the eye's or extreme colorful energy that may give you a great experience or an impression in expressionism photography.

The journey through this book is remarkable regarding the things overlooked by our eyes and it can sometimes be over examined by our own values when we forget to look at life from all angles and not just one. This can give the viewer another glance into their own path of art or even business. As they say "One step forward and two steps back." This statement has been around for centuries and still holds strong to this day and the design of the words are to keep one's own path in a focus driven outlook on life. I do believe the two steps are from the angle that are missed with the senses and this book can give you another approach of looking through your own lens from many optical points of view.

The twists of fate carry us through the good times and even at the worst of times and in these moments, we sometimes can carry a heavy burden within us and never know it or we can inspire others to grow with this good feeling to those in need around us. I am giving this impression of inspiration to those of in need and to enrich the ones on whom already inspire people on their daily life.

Life is always moving and changing in this world and my overall glance at my expressionism photography is to express the passion in your heart and give you a journey of hope for something better within your own footprints on this earth. May life take you on a better journey and expressionism within your own voice of reason and make a better world for our next generation.

American Artist

Expressionism Photography

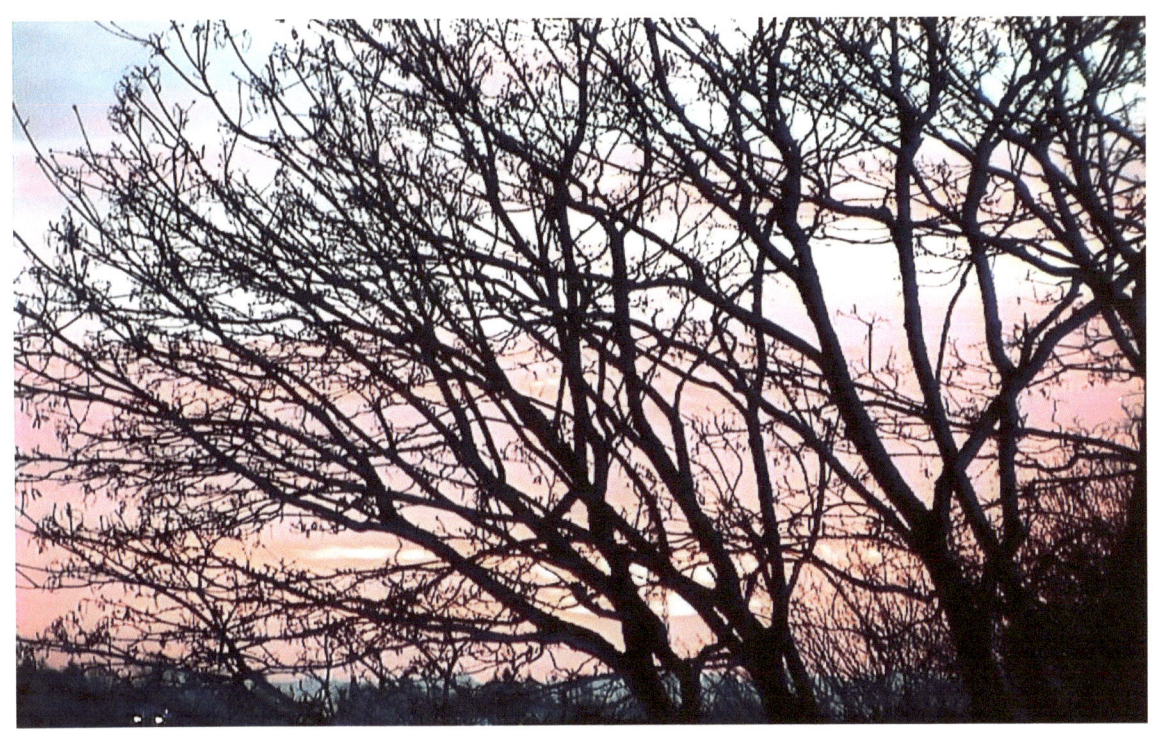

Seeing Love

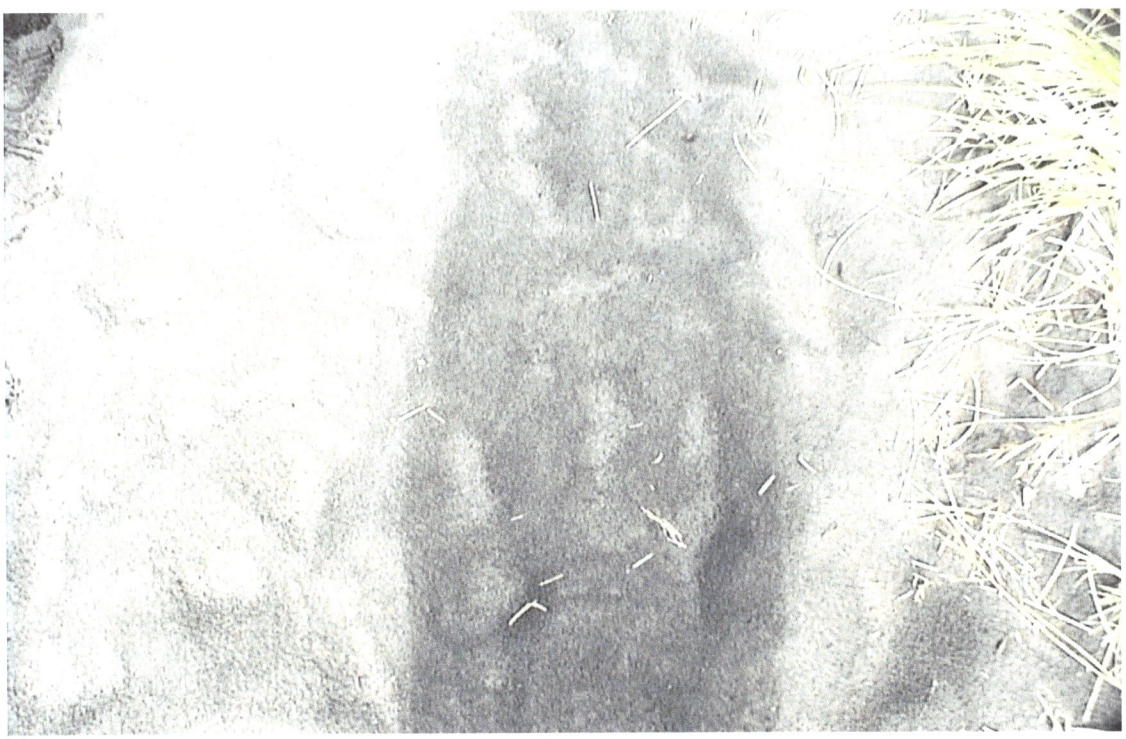

Soft Texture

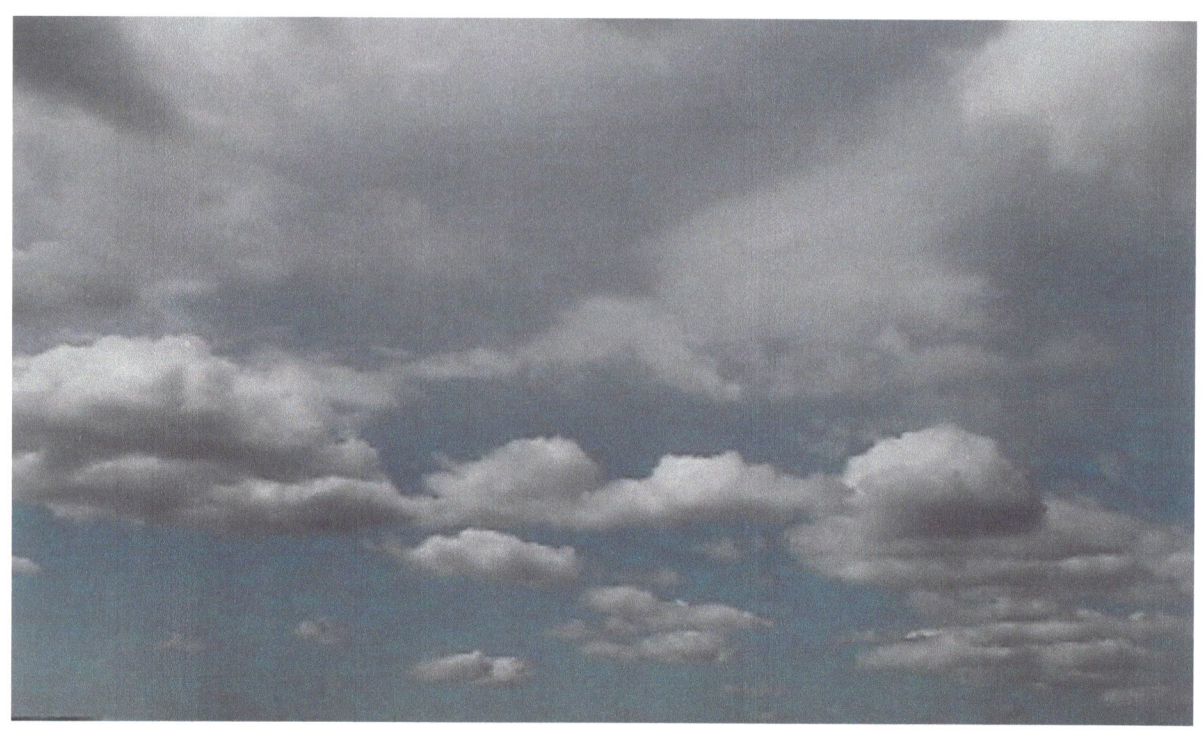

Captured In-Love

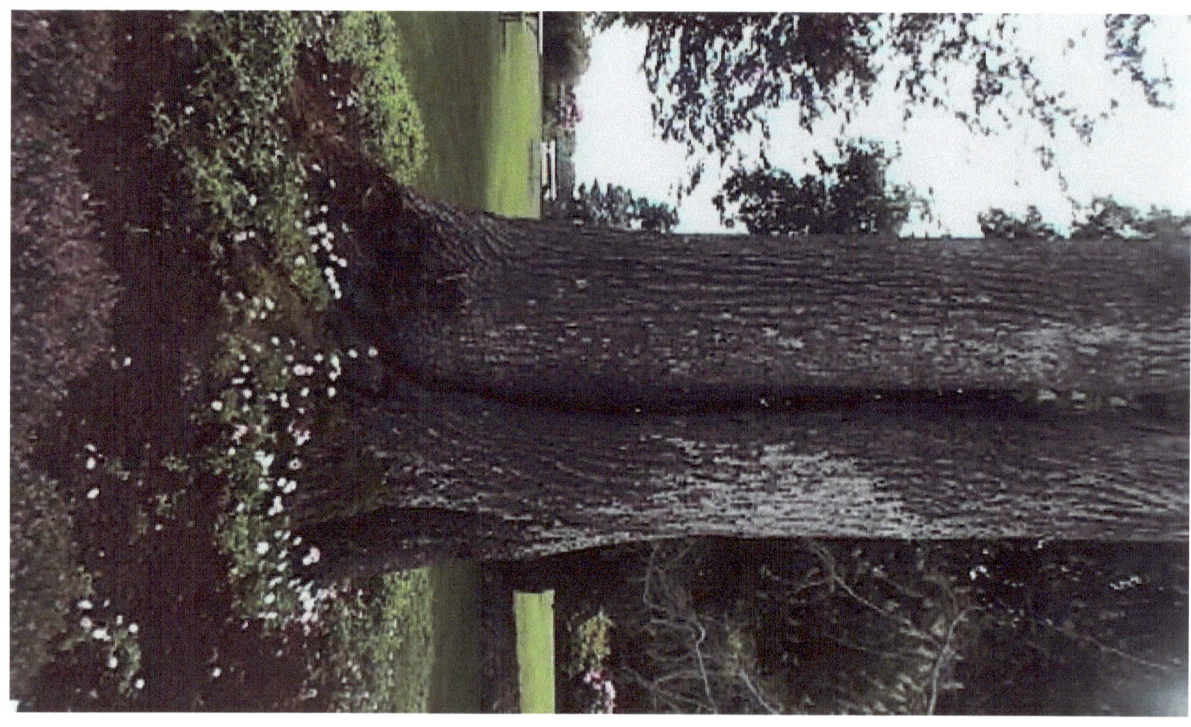

Logically Seeing Roots

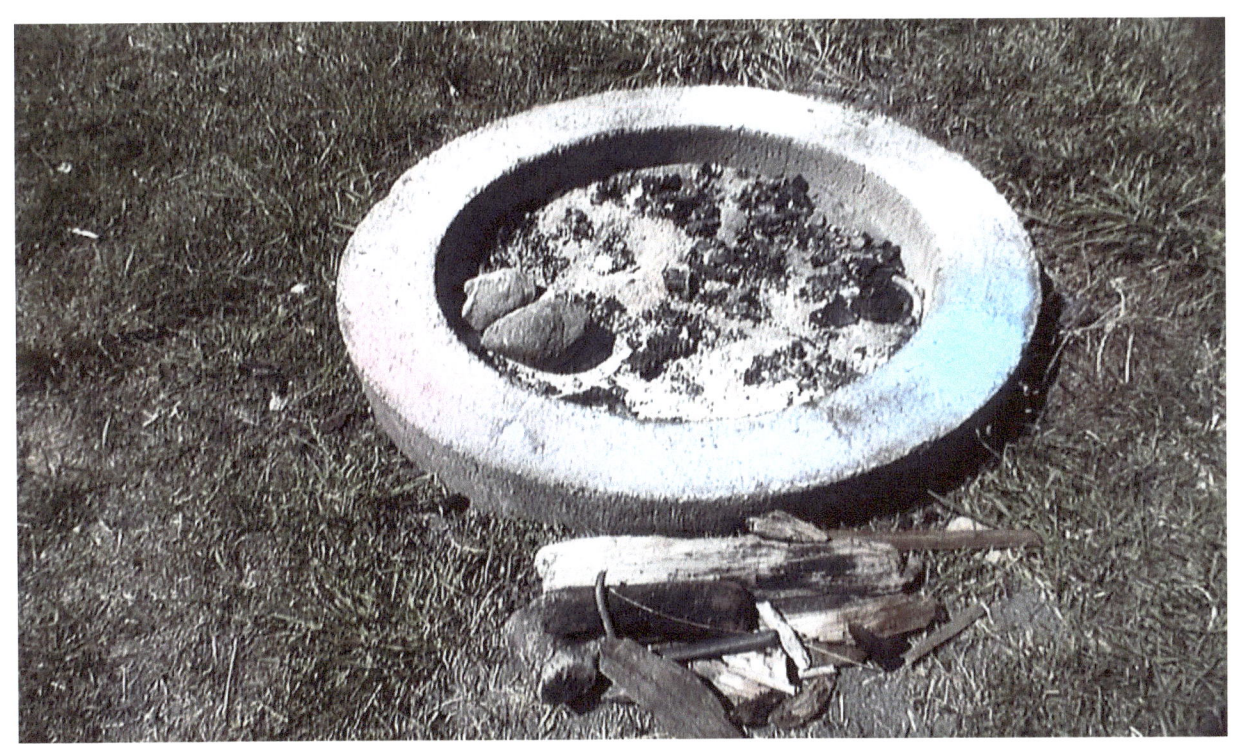

Gloss Colors

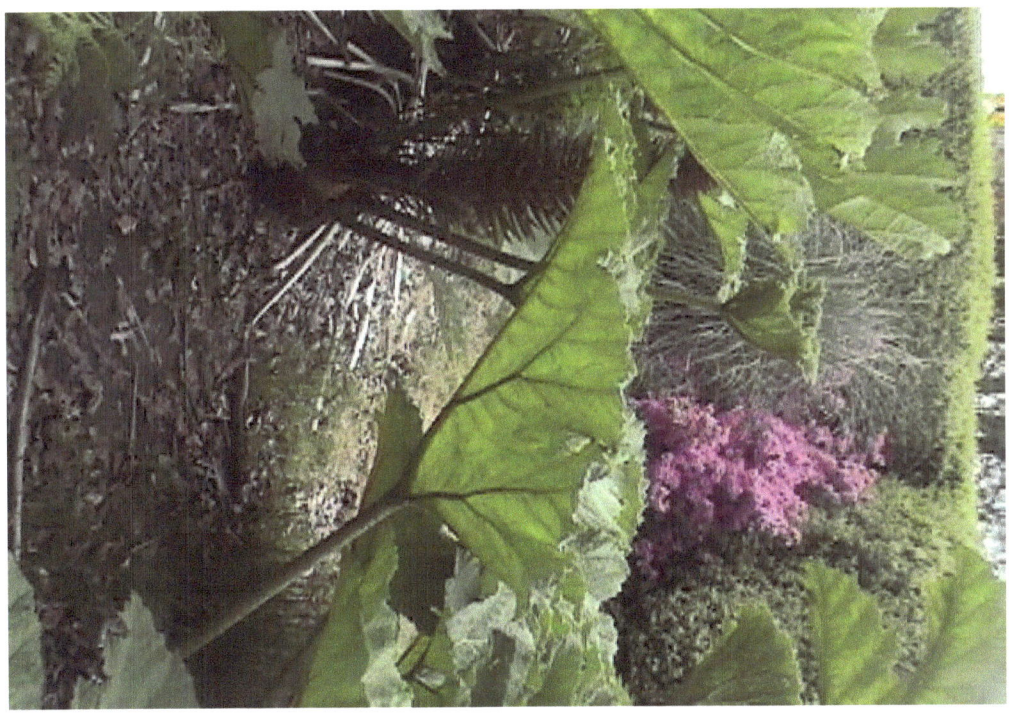

Integrative Angle

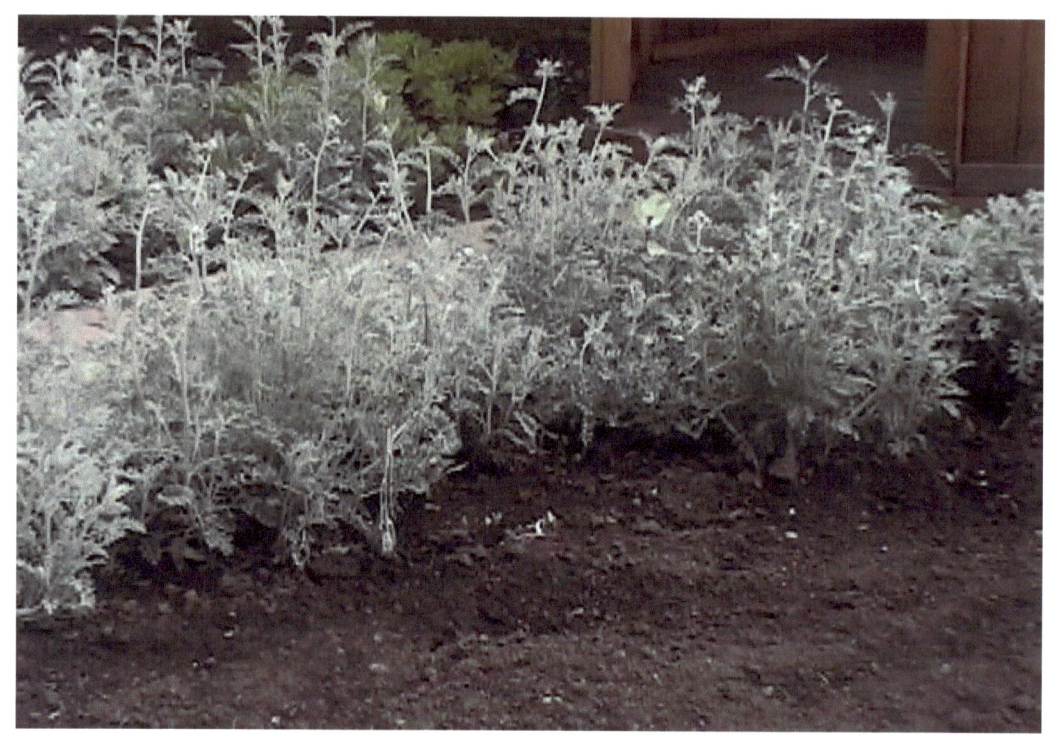

Electricity

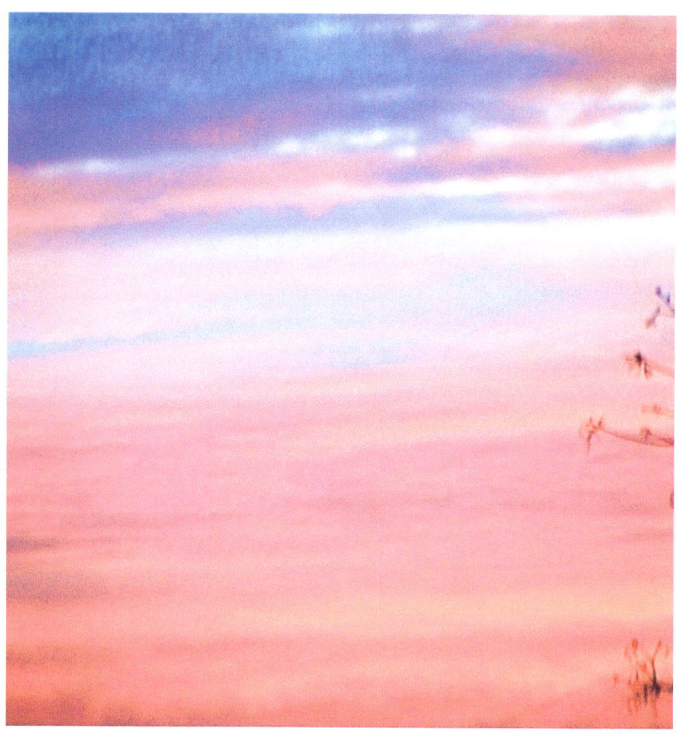

Glaze

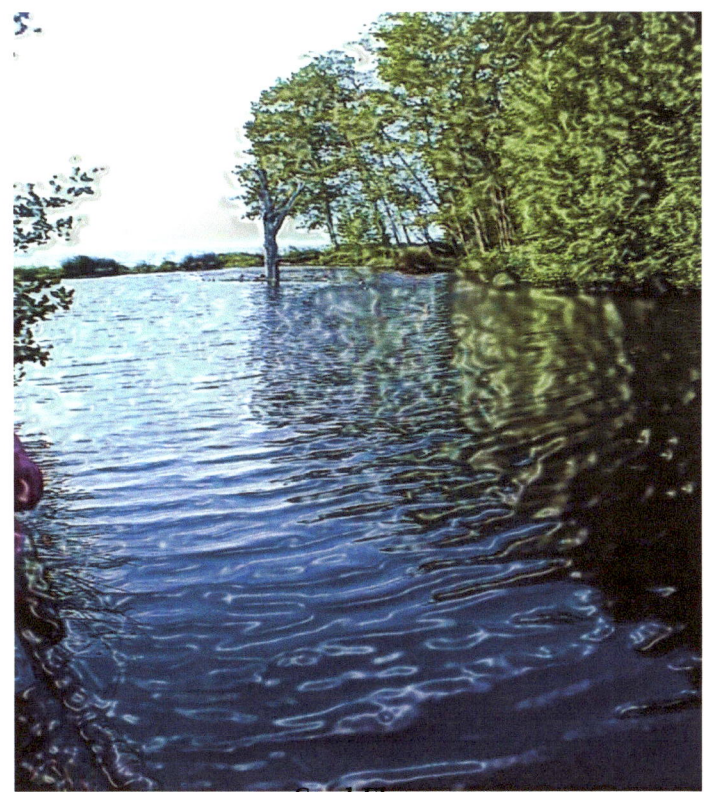
Soul Flow

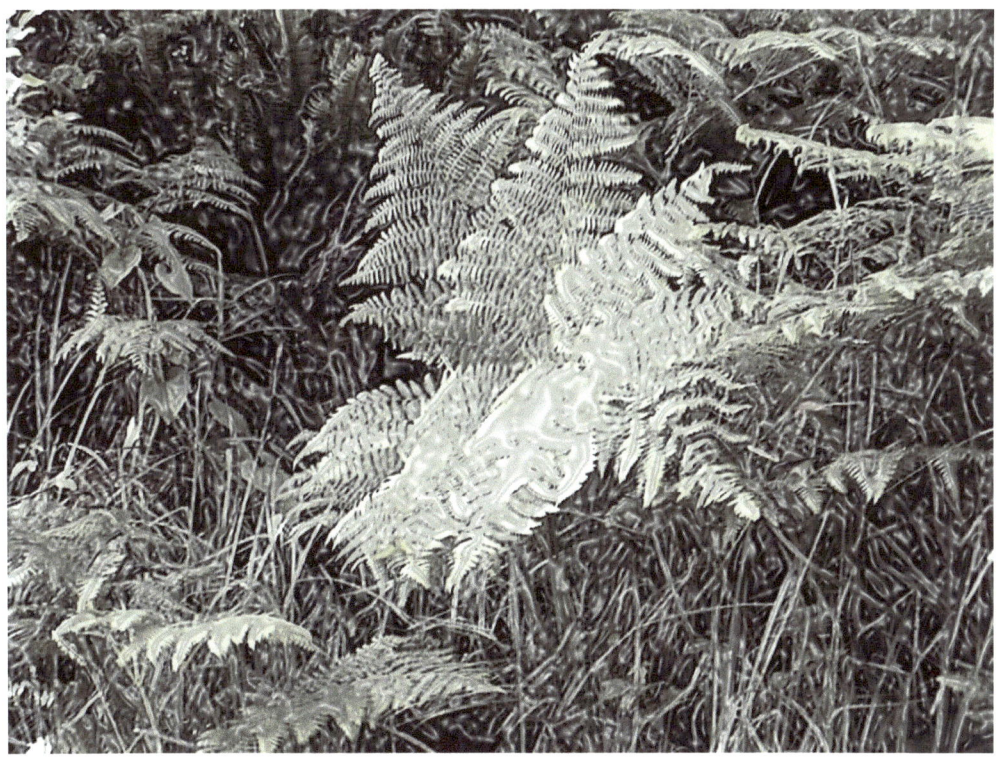
New Oneness

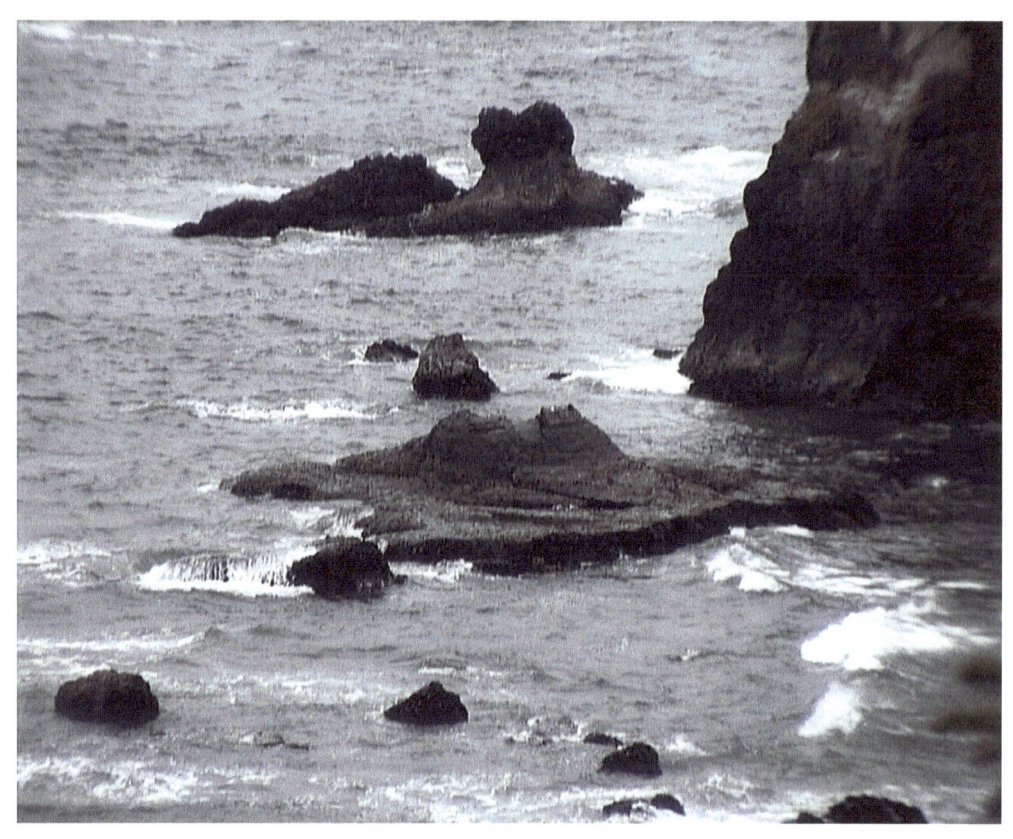
Salty Rocks

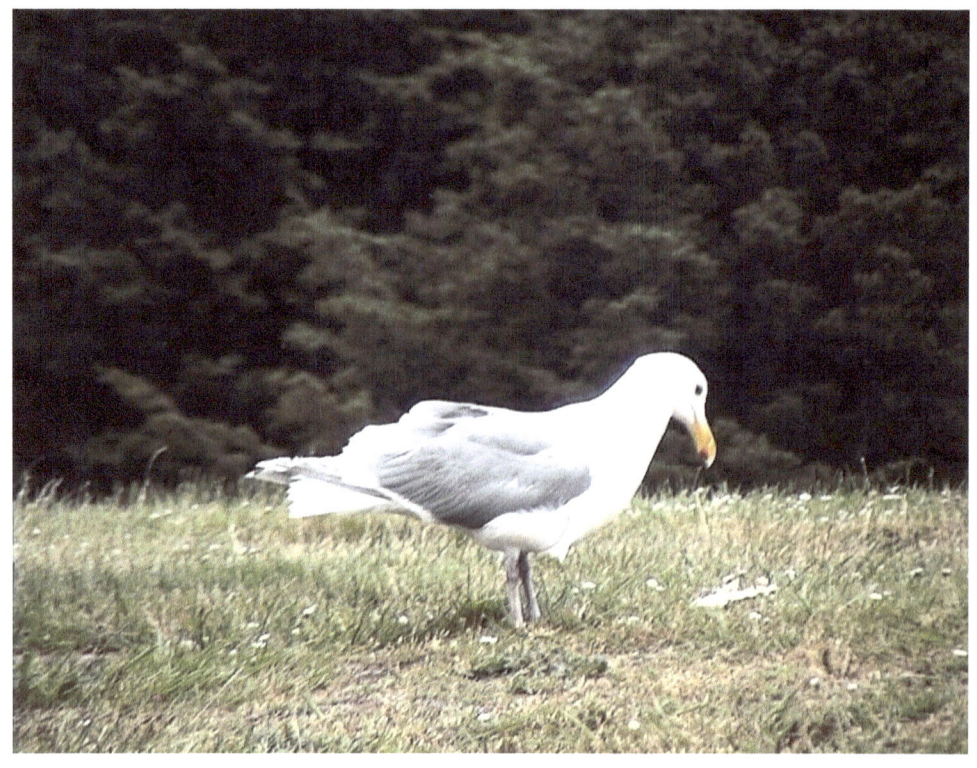
Energy Glow

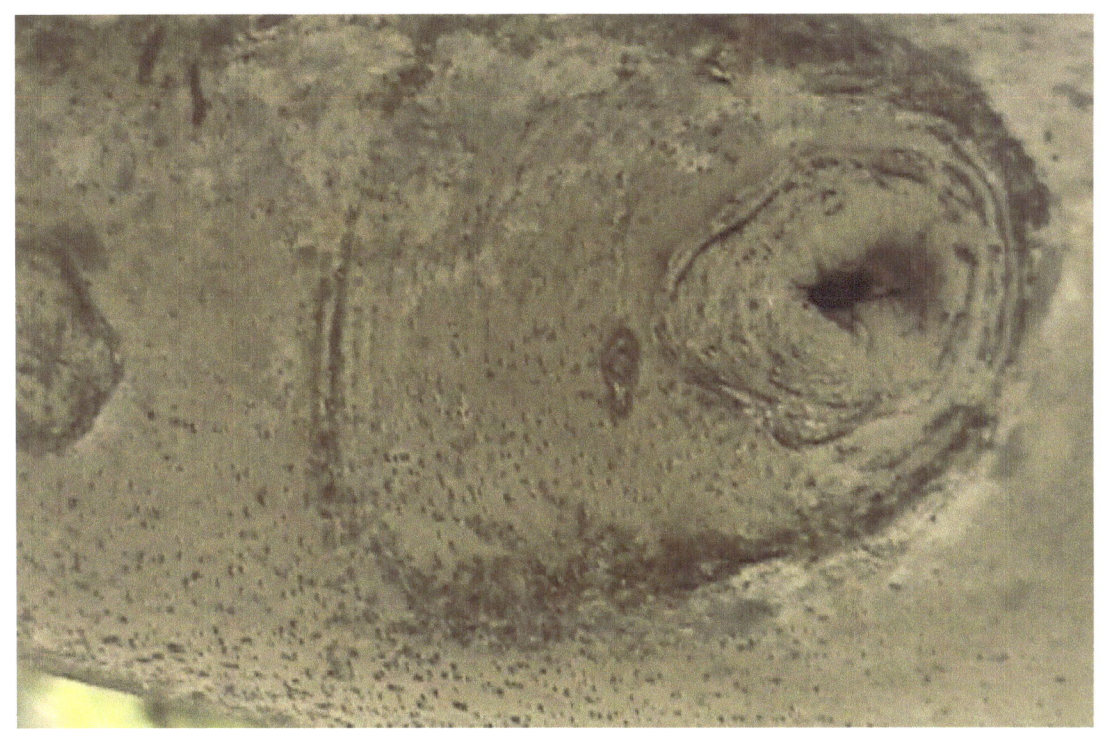

Tiny Opening

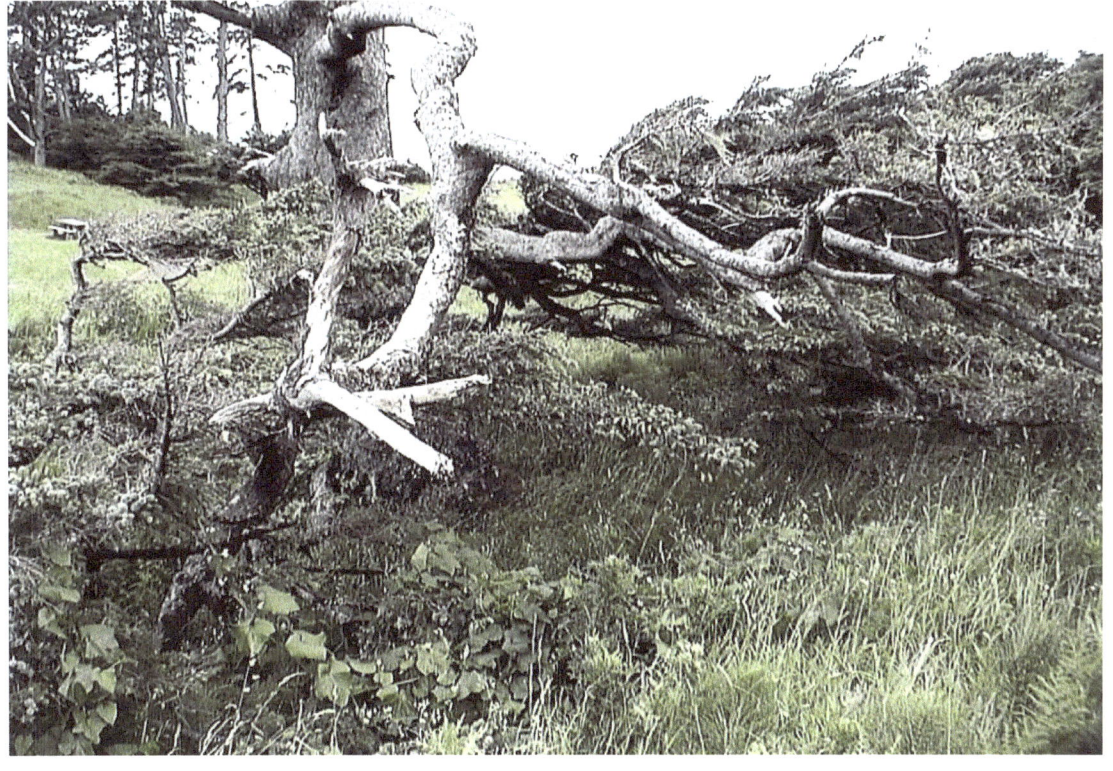

Layers Beneath

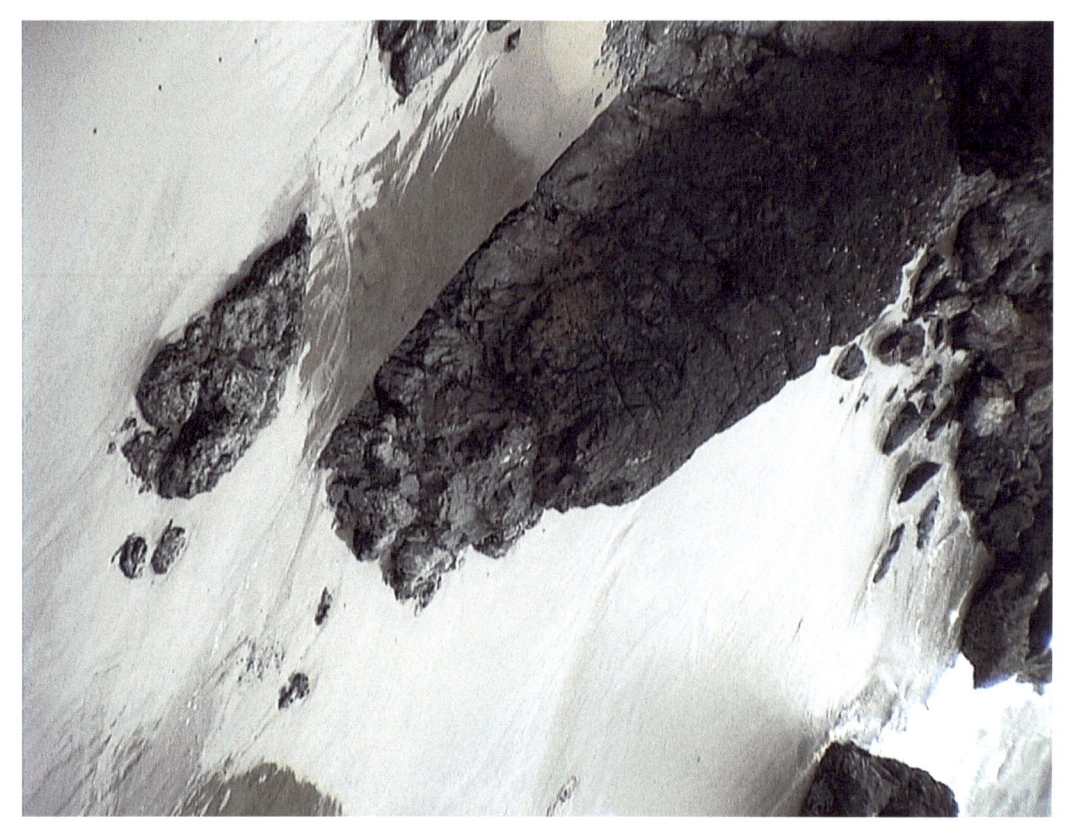

Glass Rock

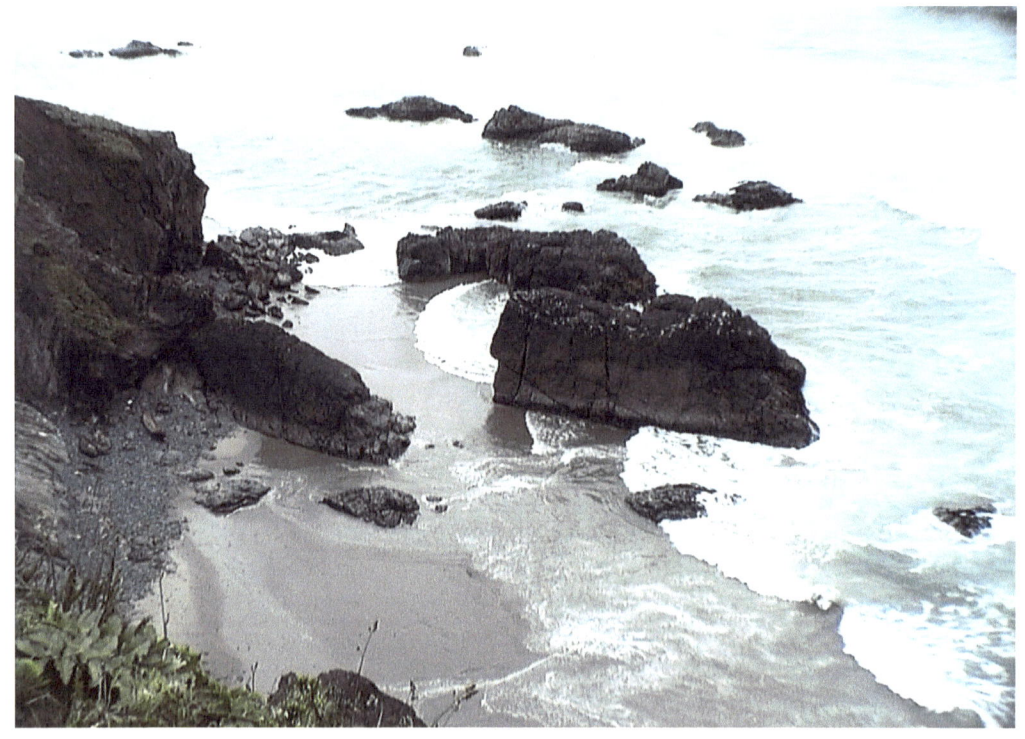

On High

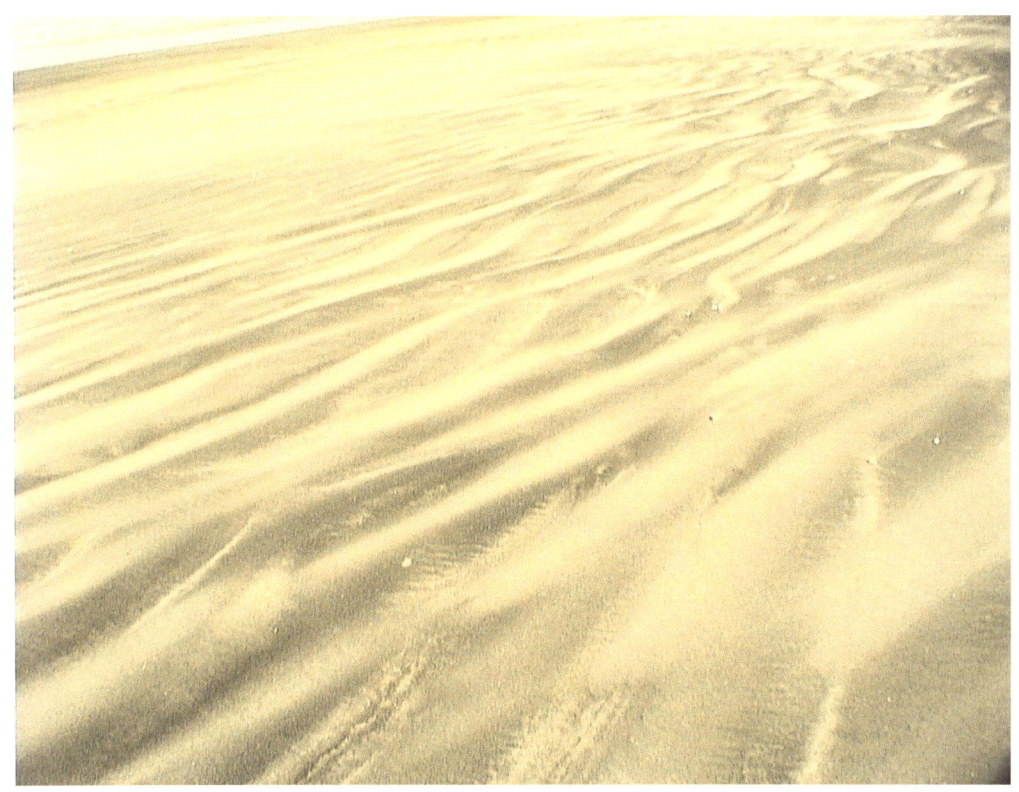

Harmony

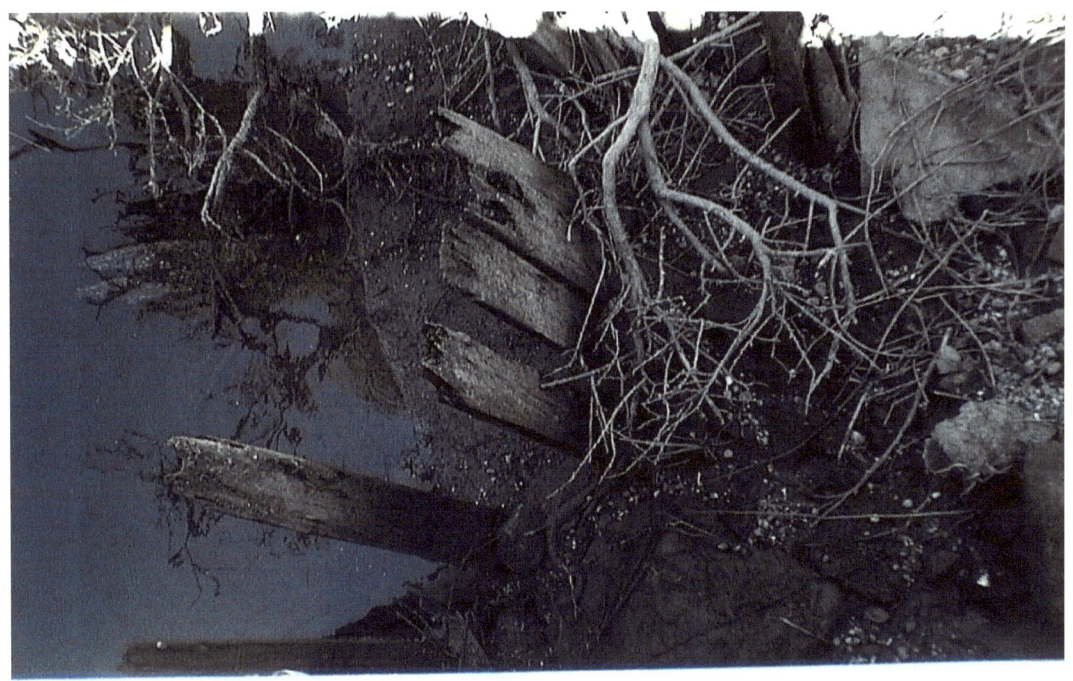

Brokenness

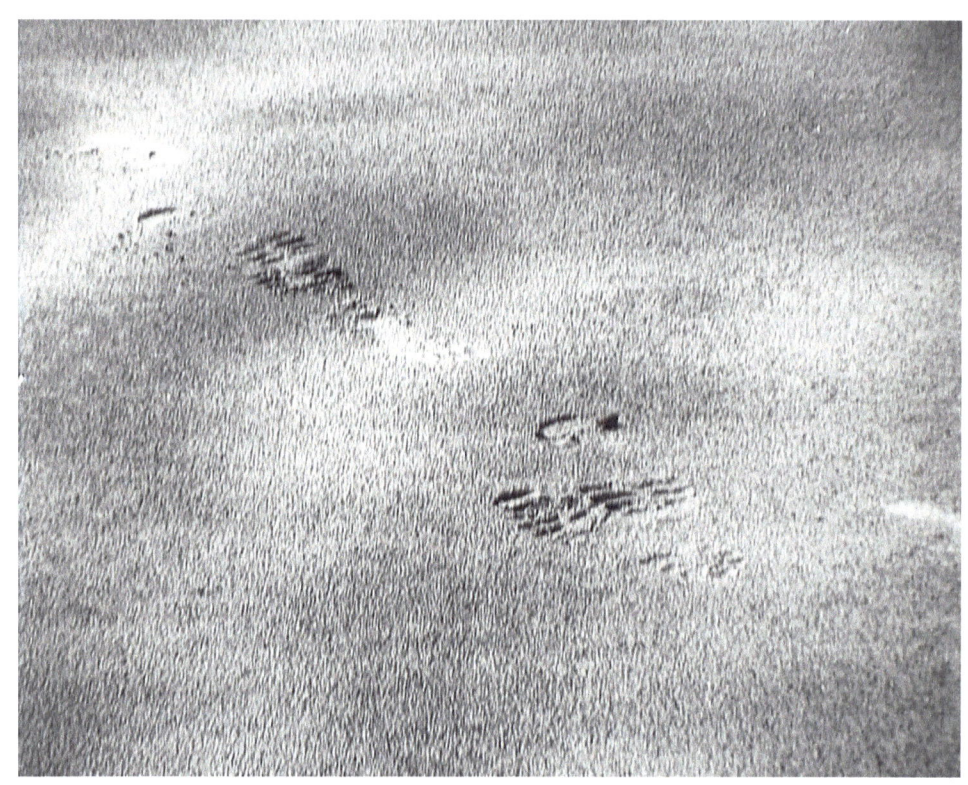

Alone

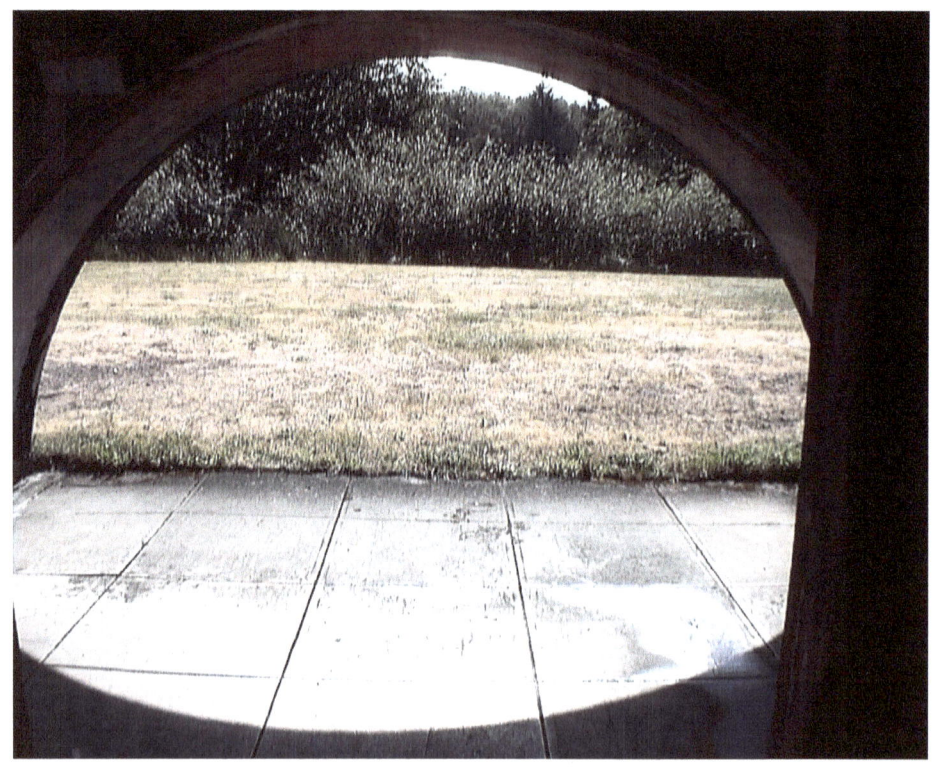

Opening Up

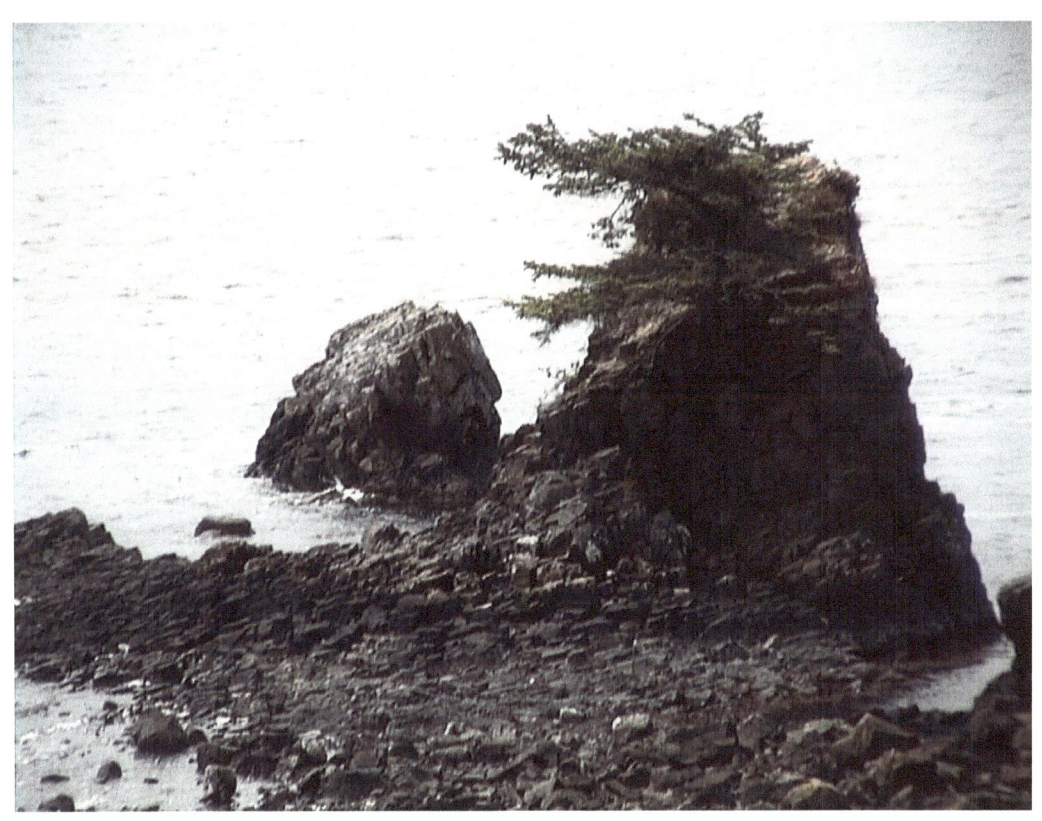

Face Expression

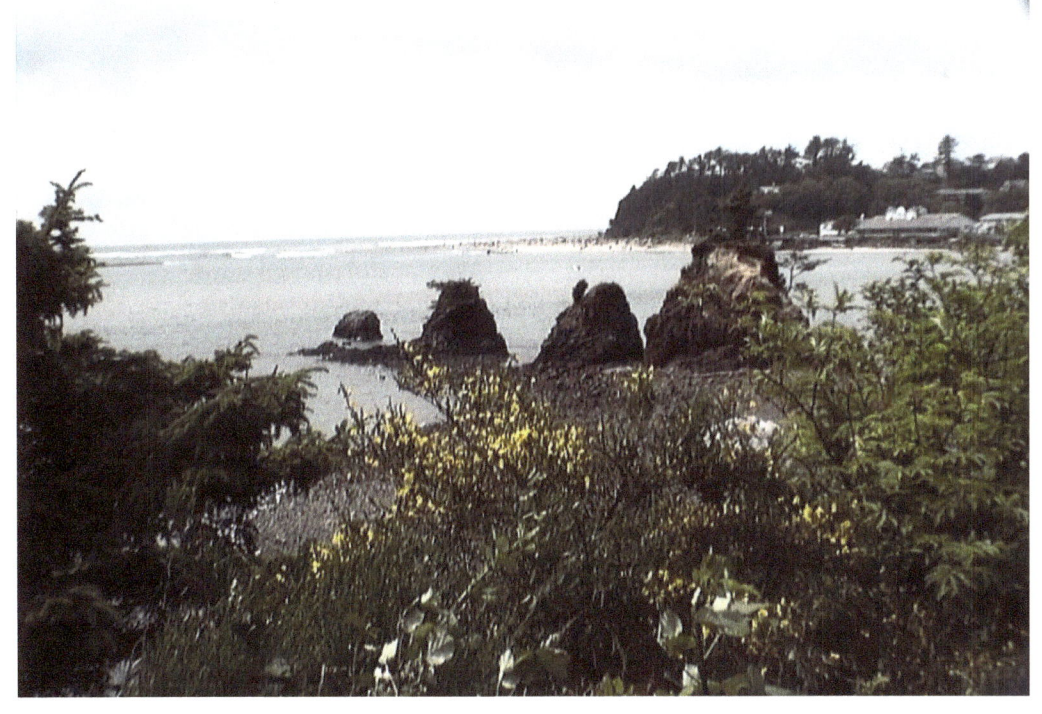

Four Signals

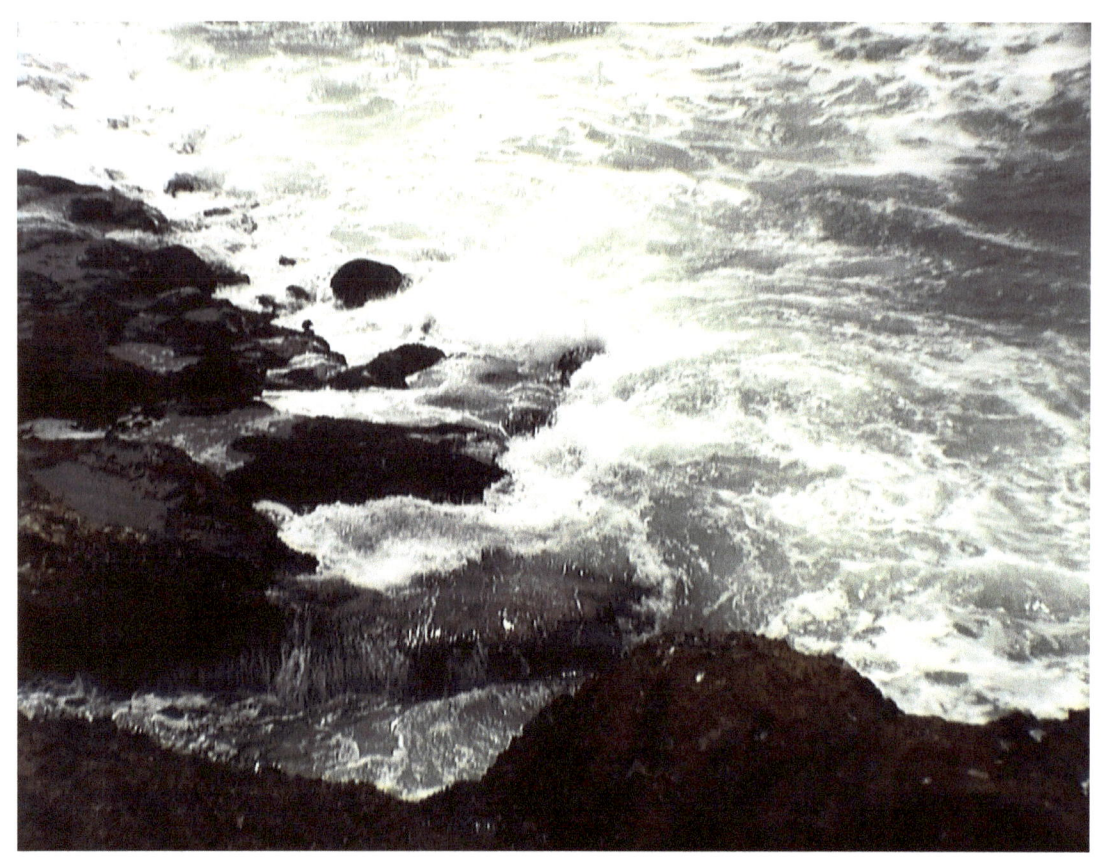

Breathe

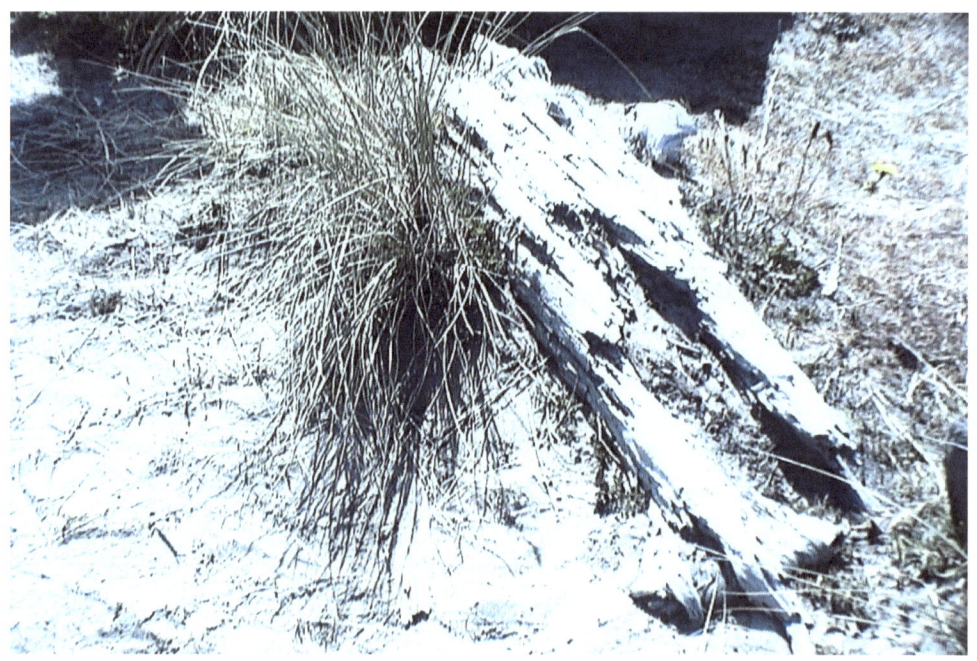

Legs

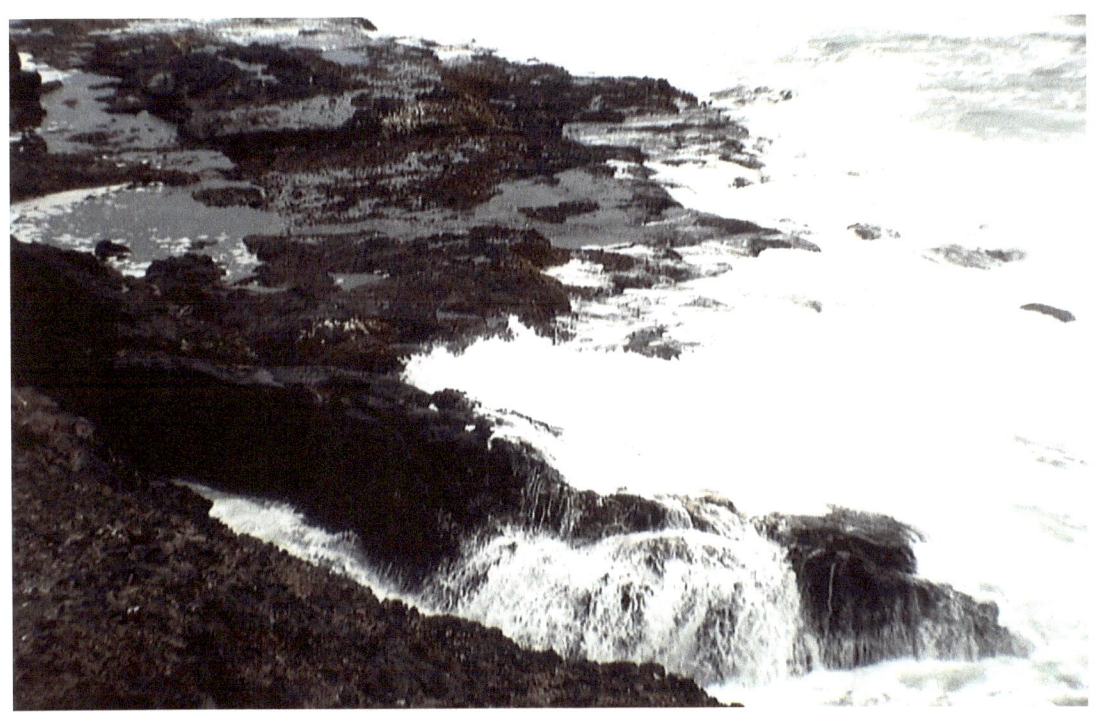

Flowing of Life

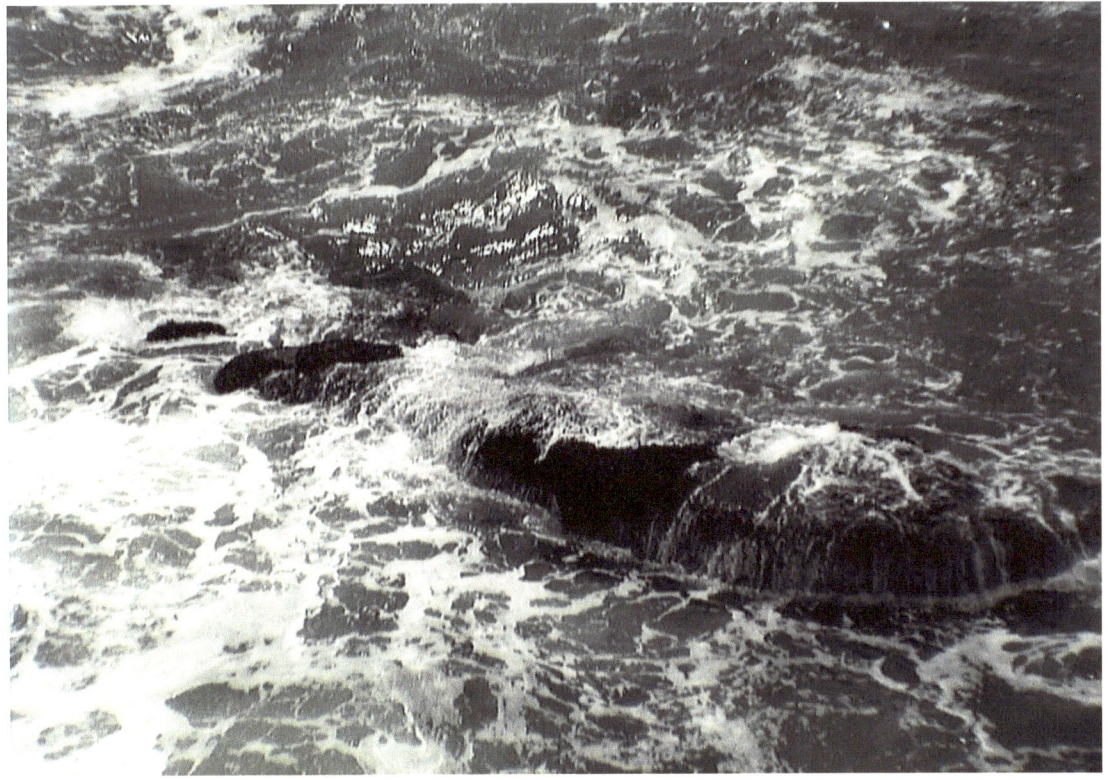

Swimming Channel

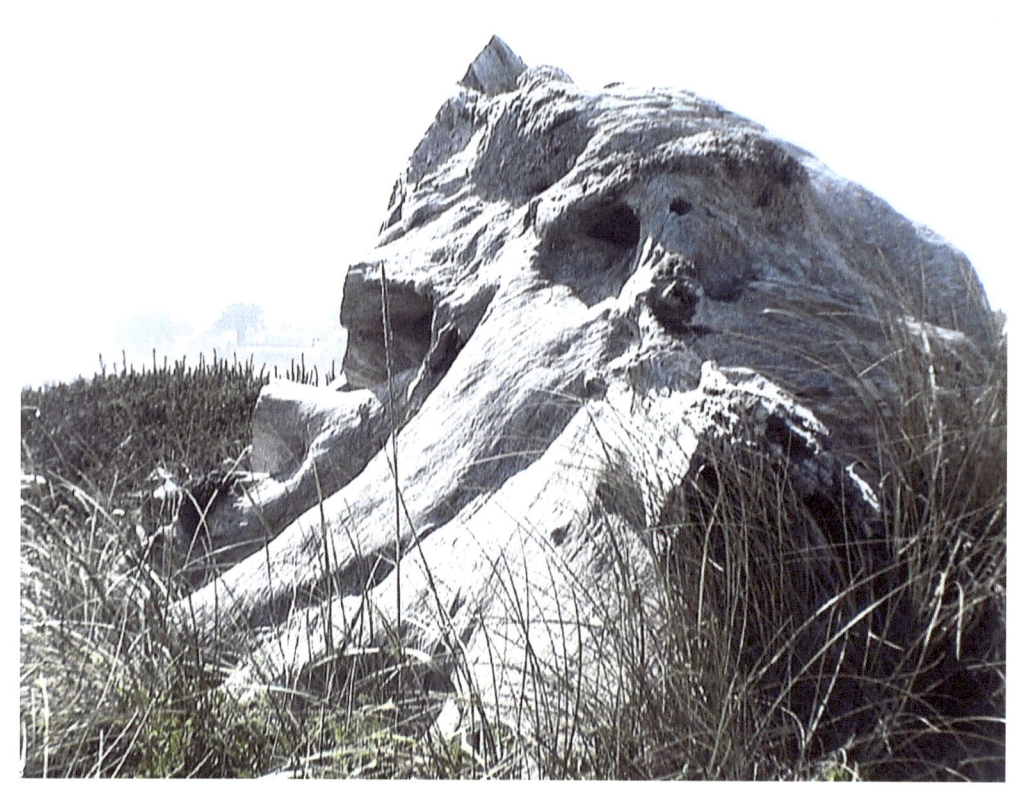

Elephant

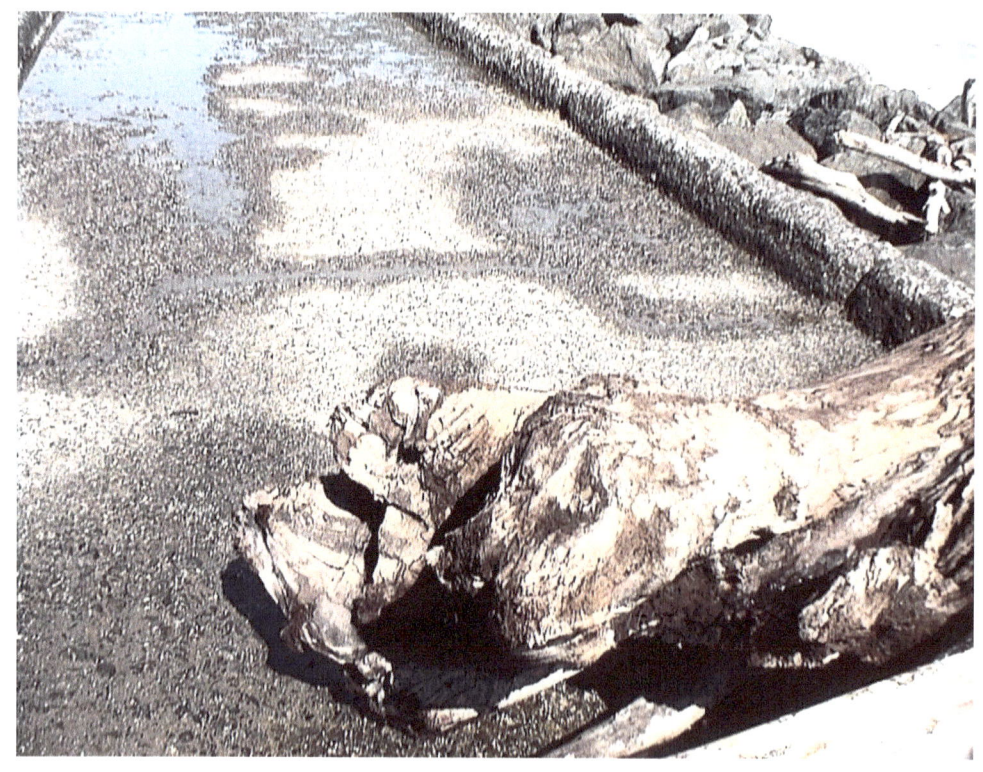

Solider

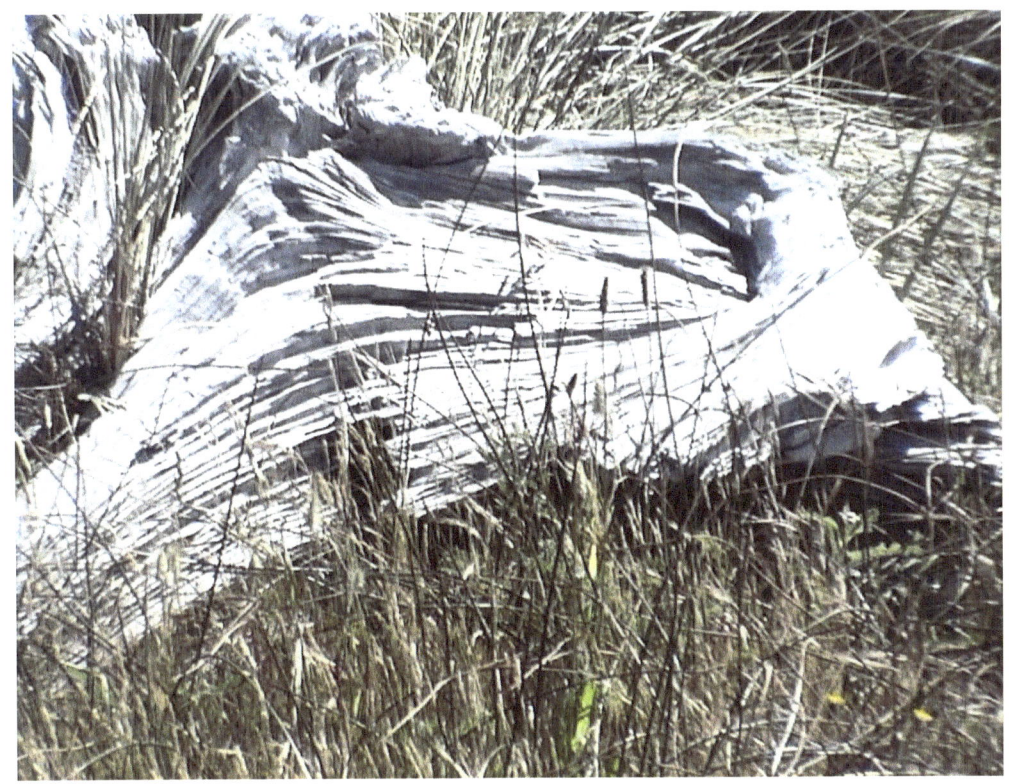

Fine Lines

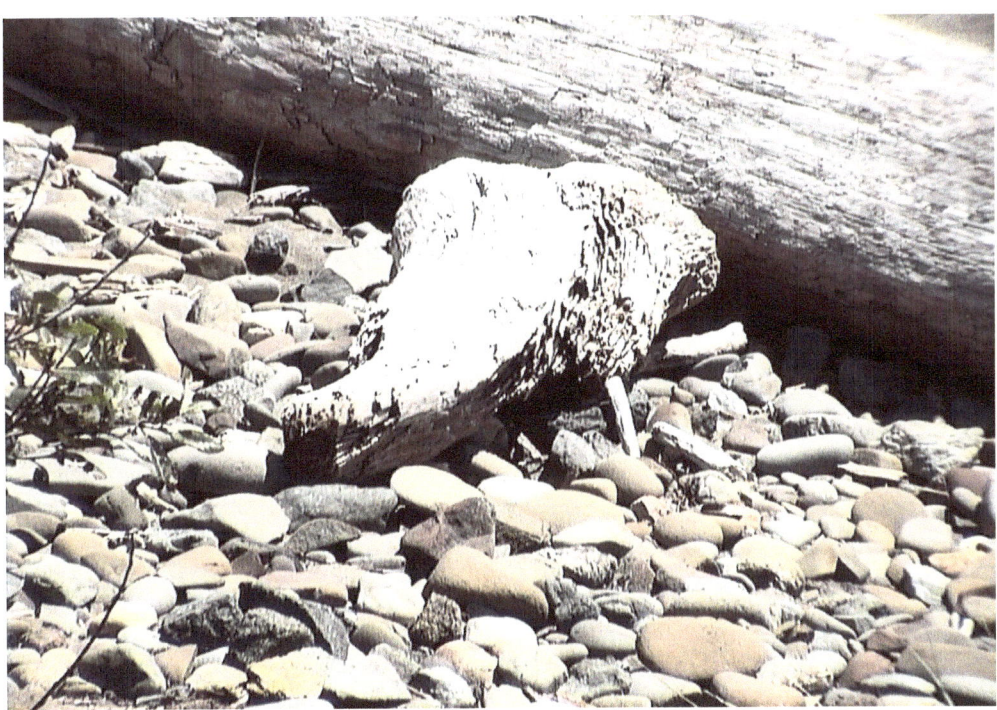

Laying Down

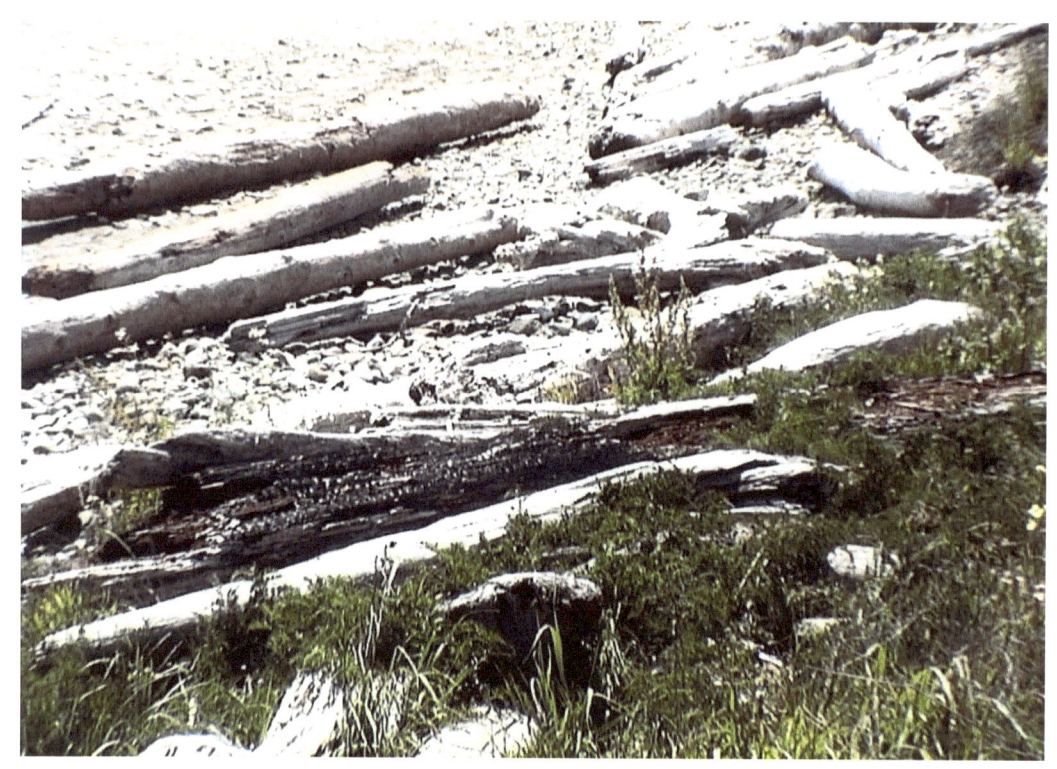

Lifting up life

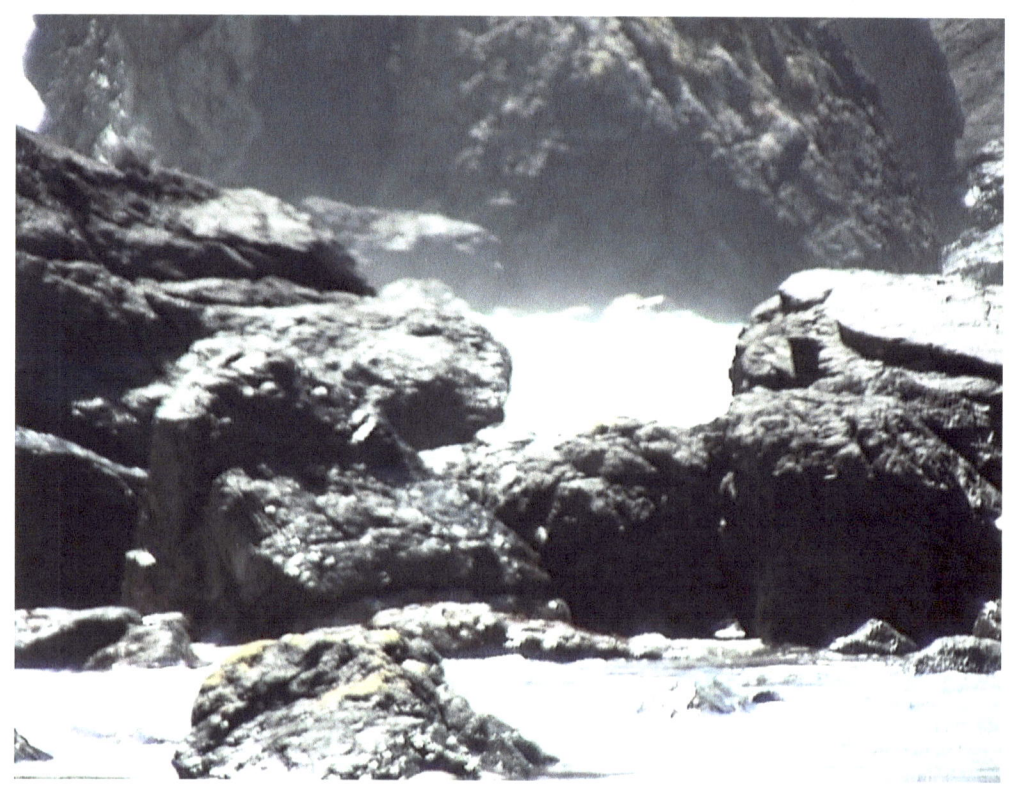

Mist Stand

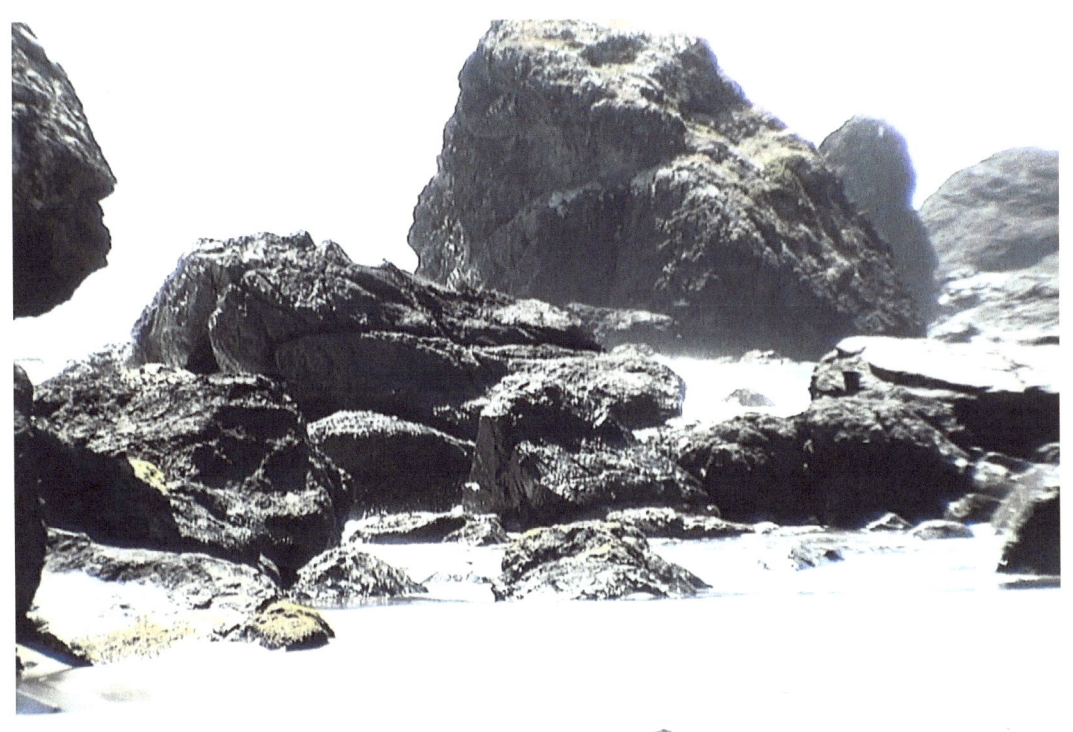

Strength Within

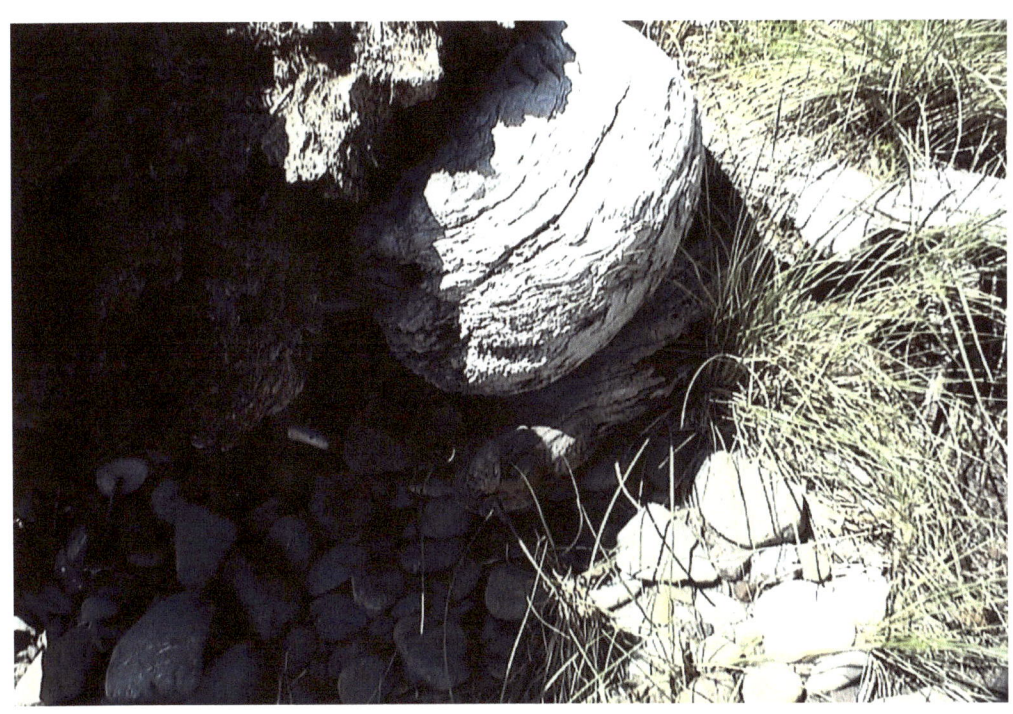

Hiding

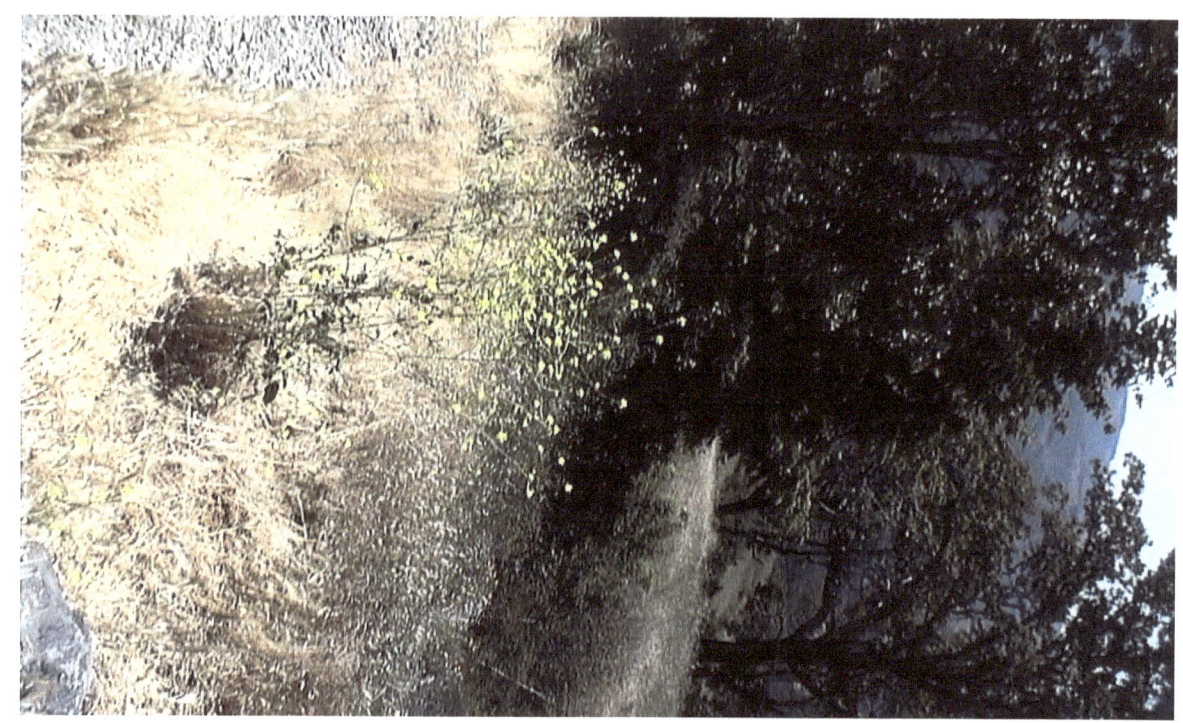

Pushing silk Love

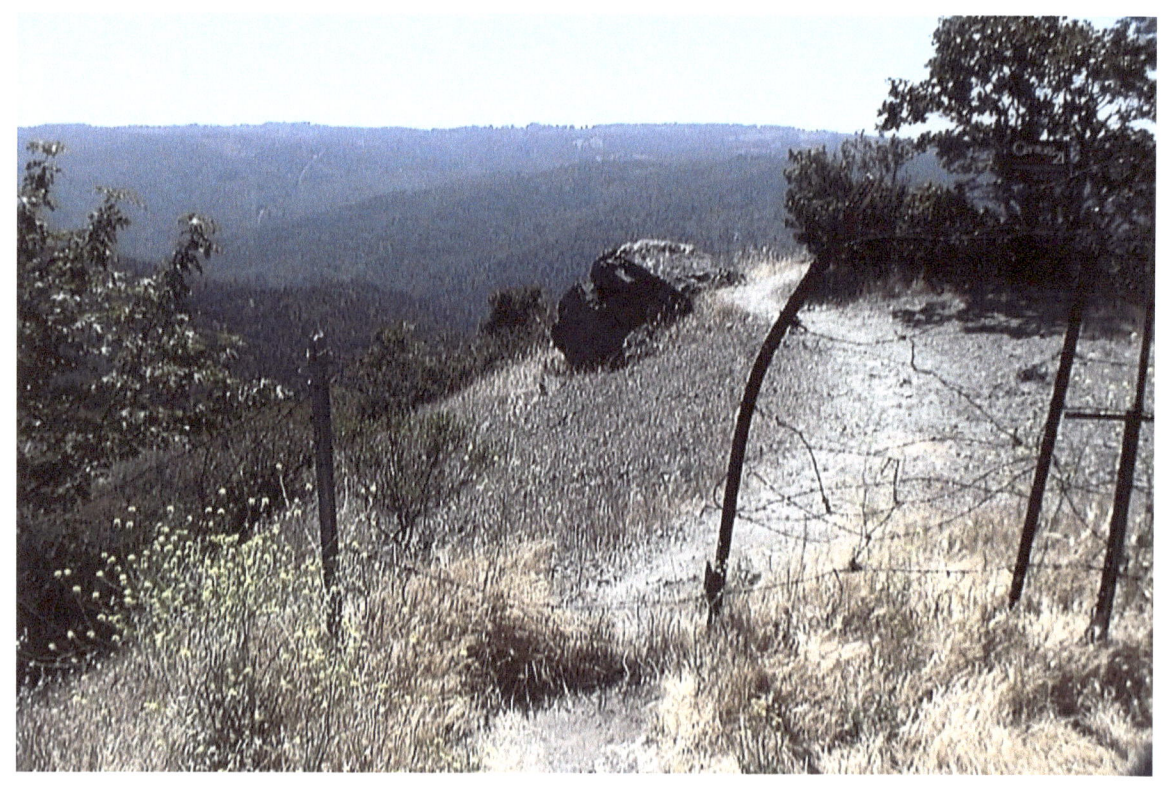

Walking through

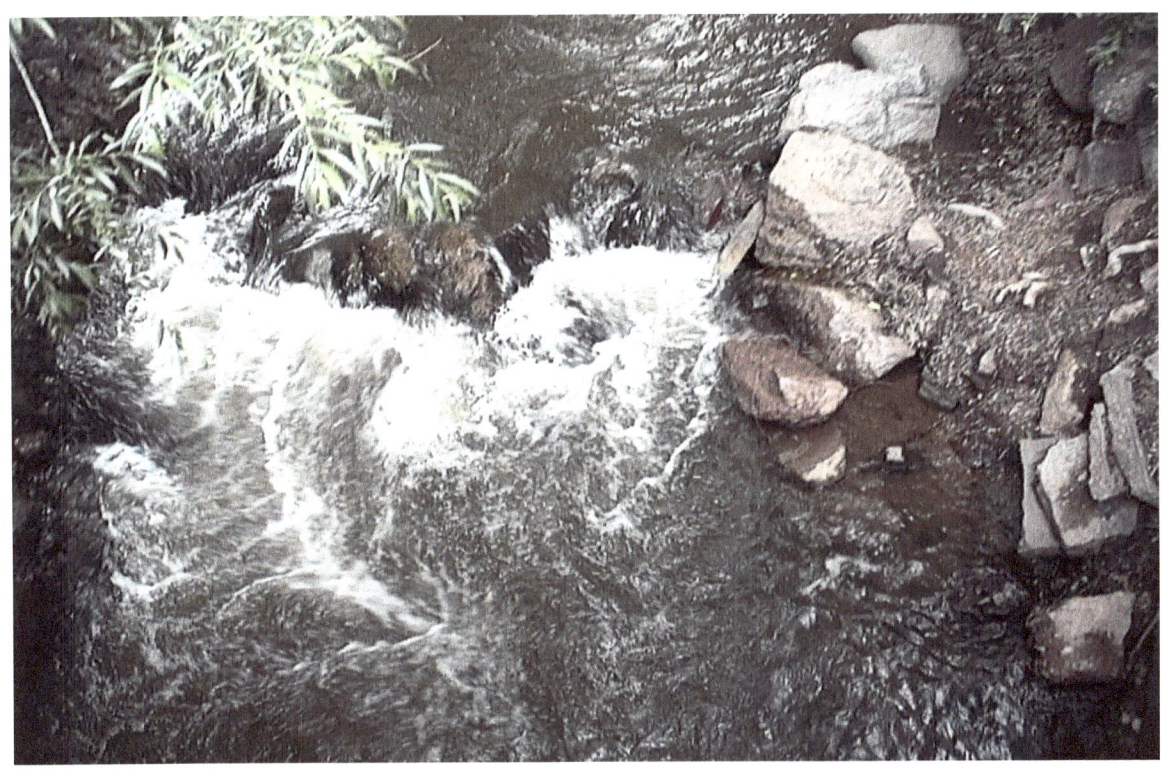

Faces

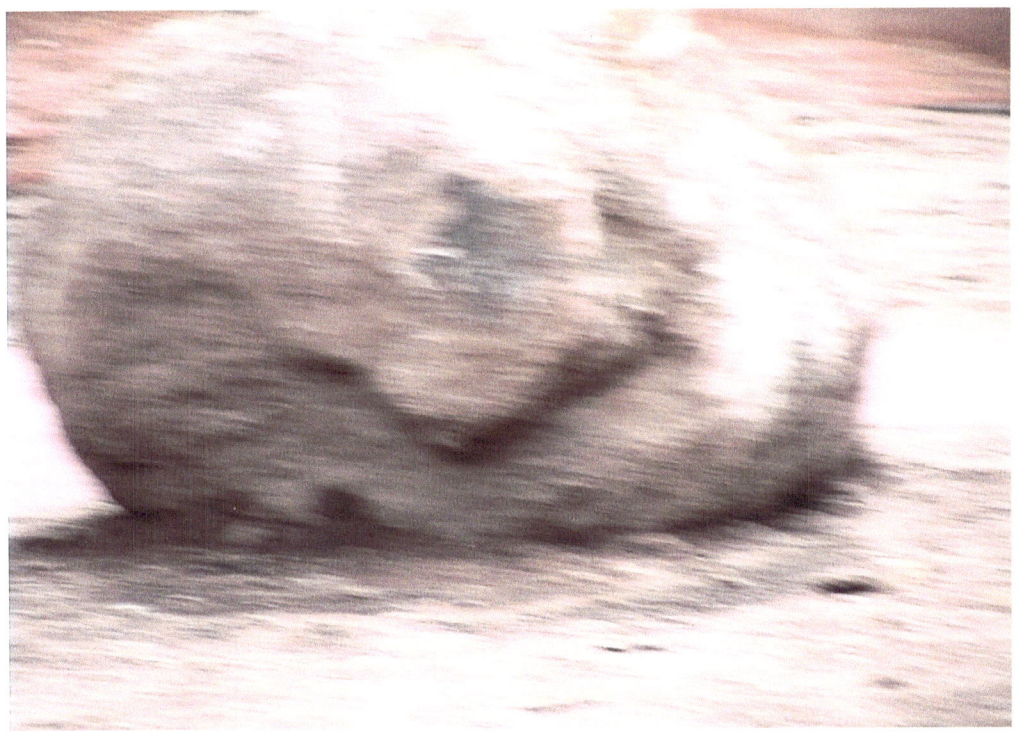

Time Movement

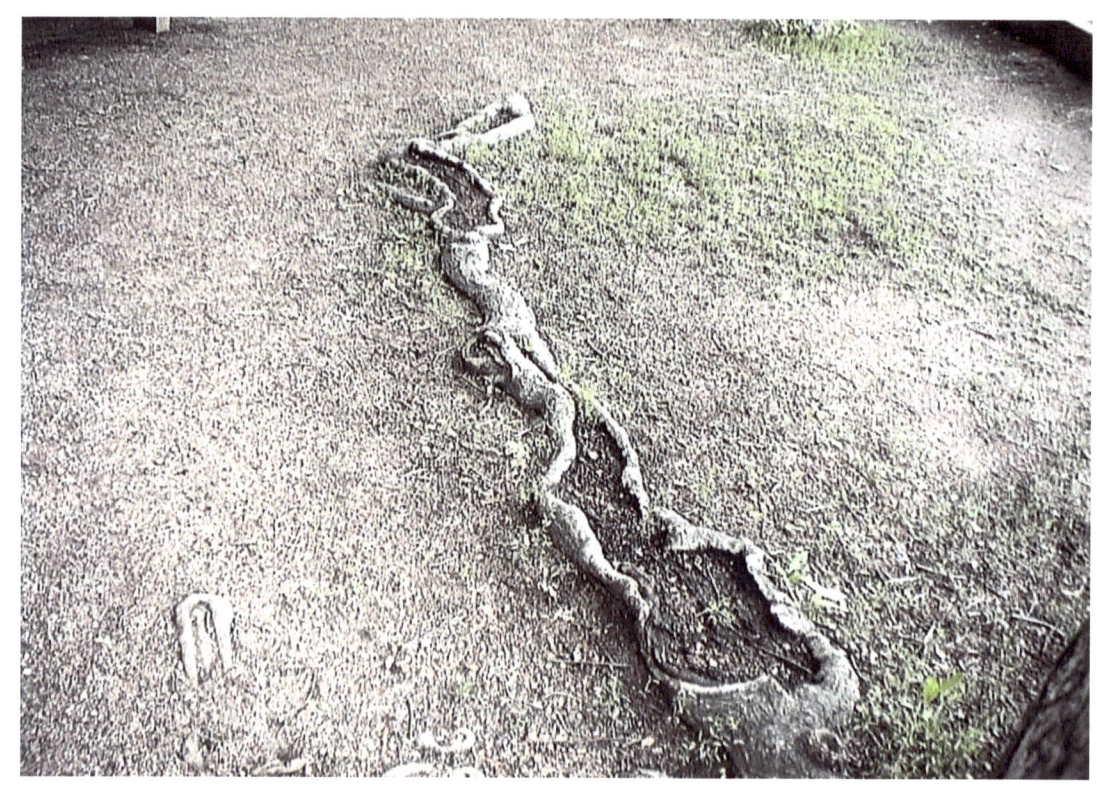

Cuddled Earth

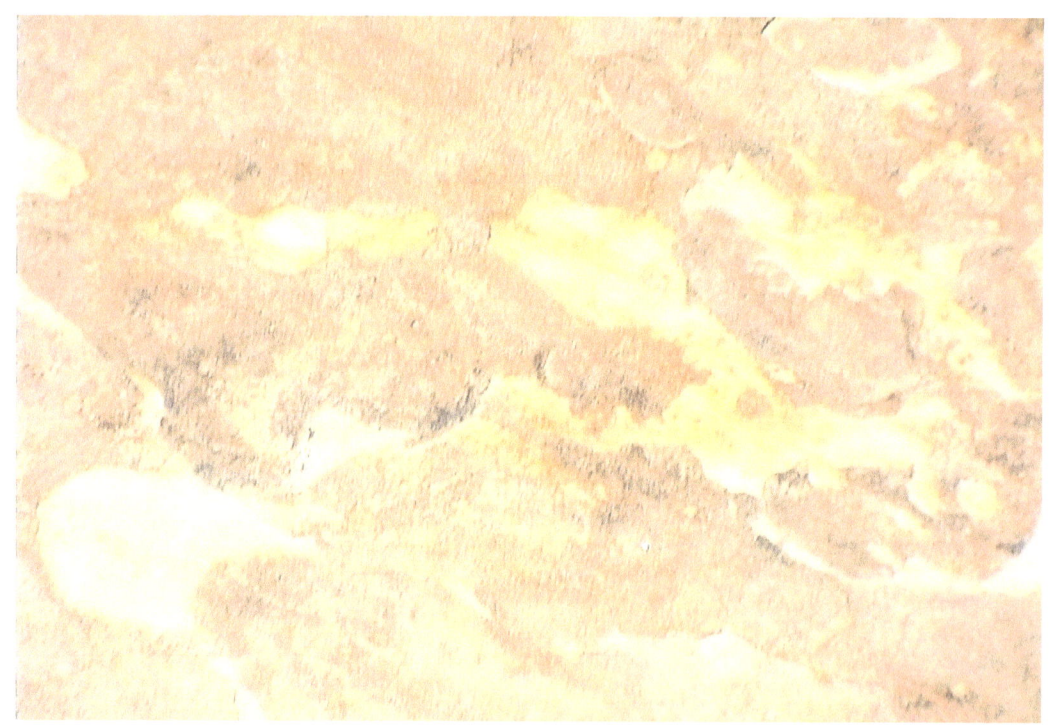

Yellow softness

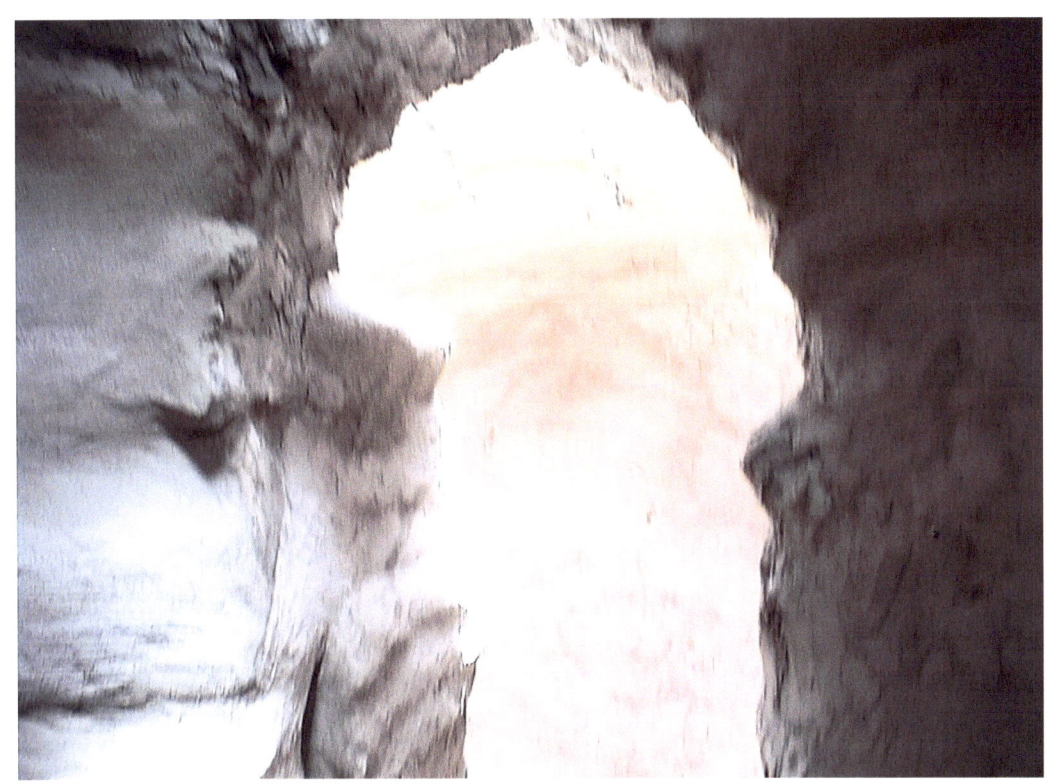

Sentimental Cave

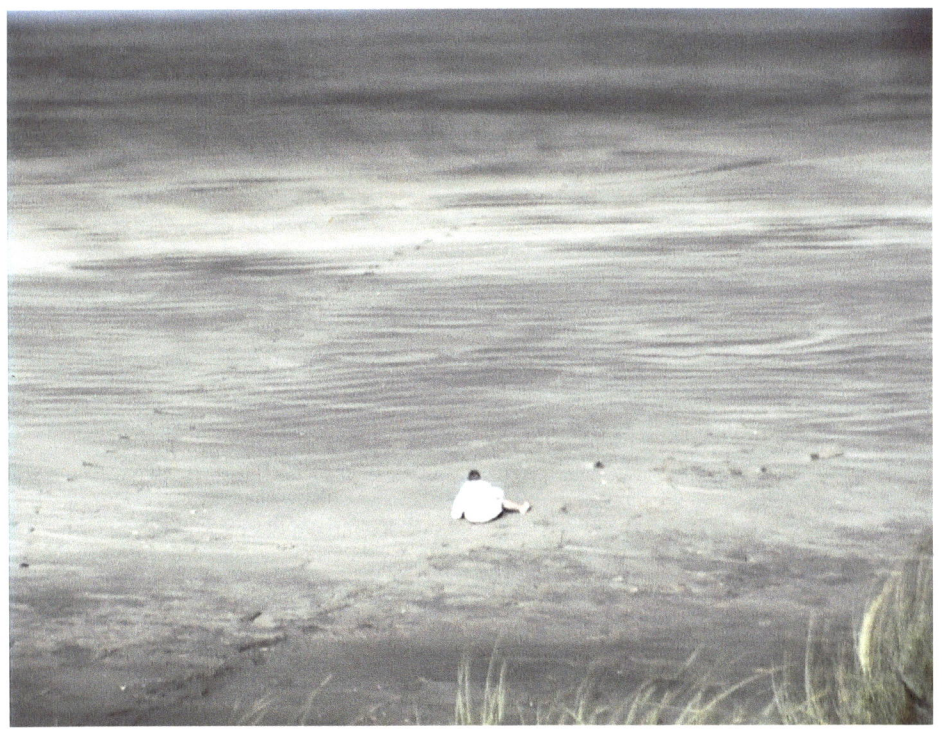

Ripples

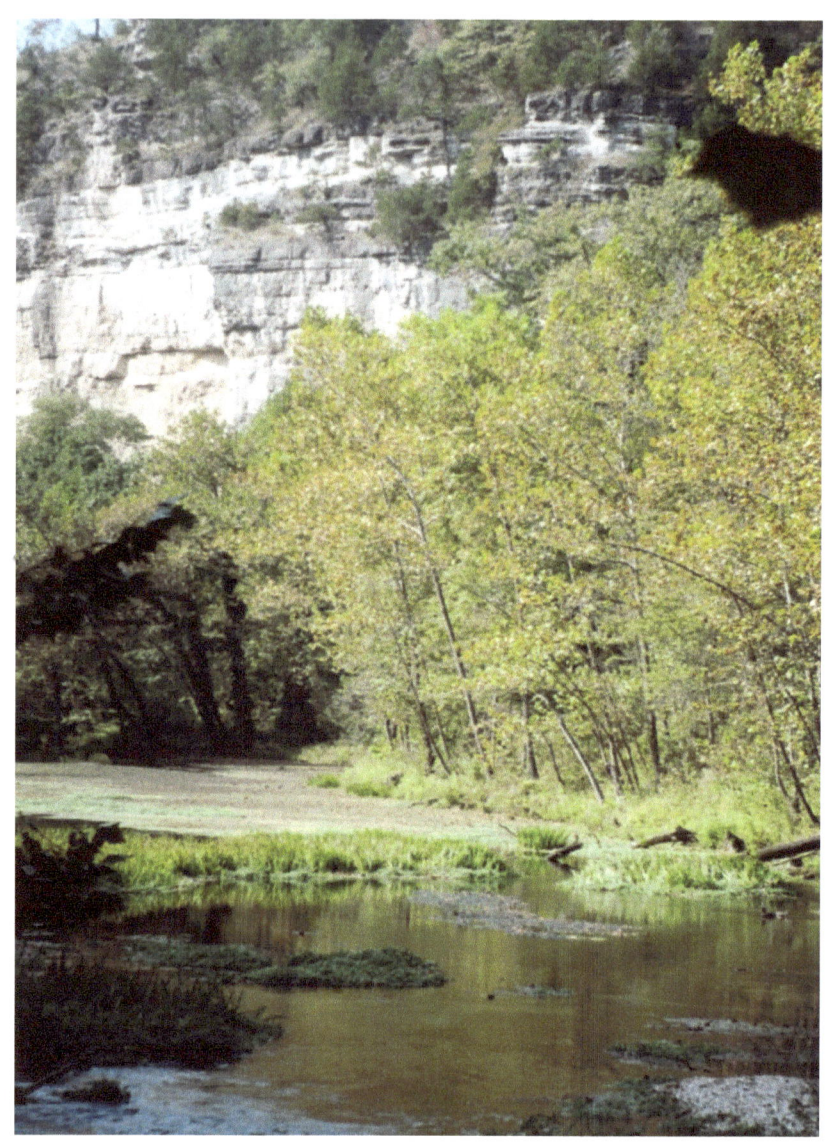

Mountain High

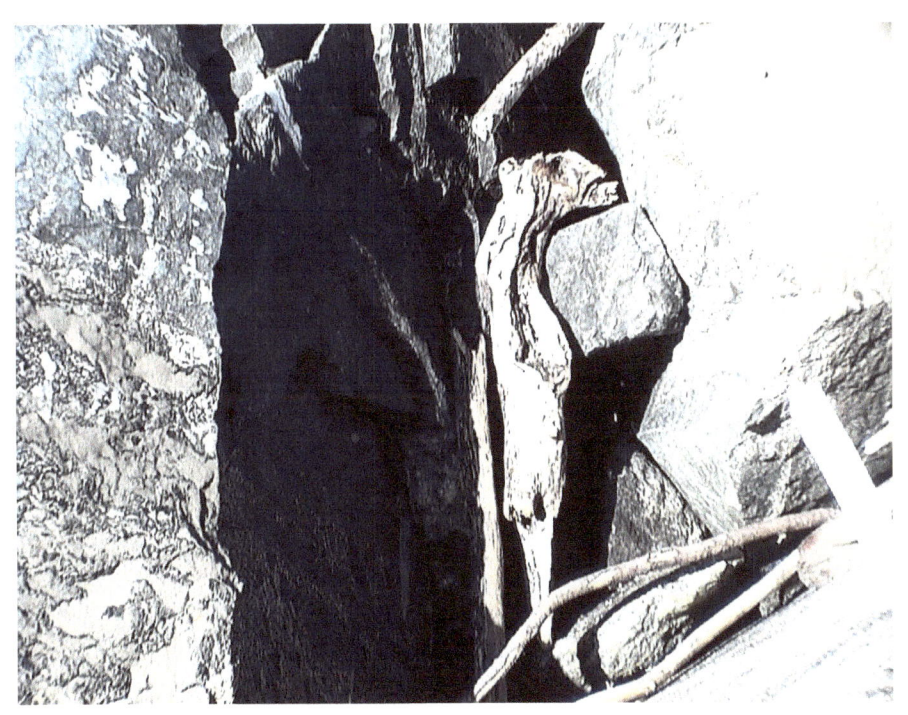

Shadow

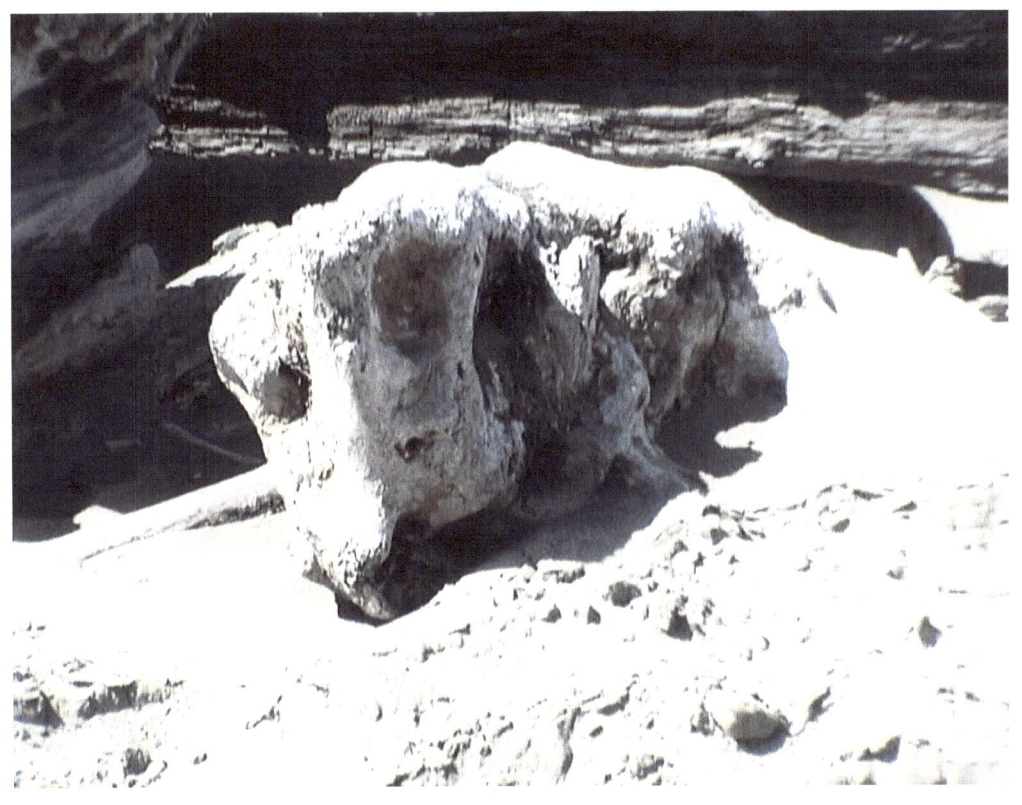

Bull

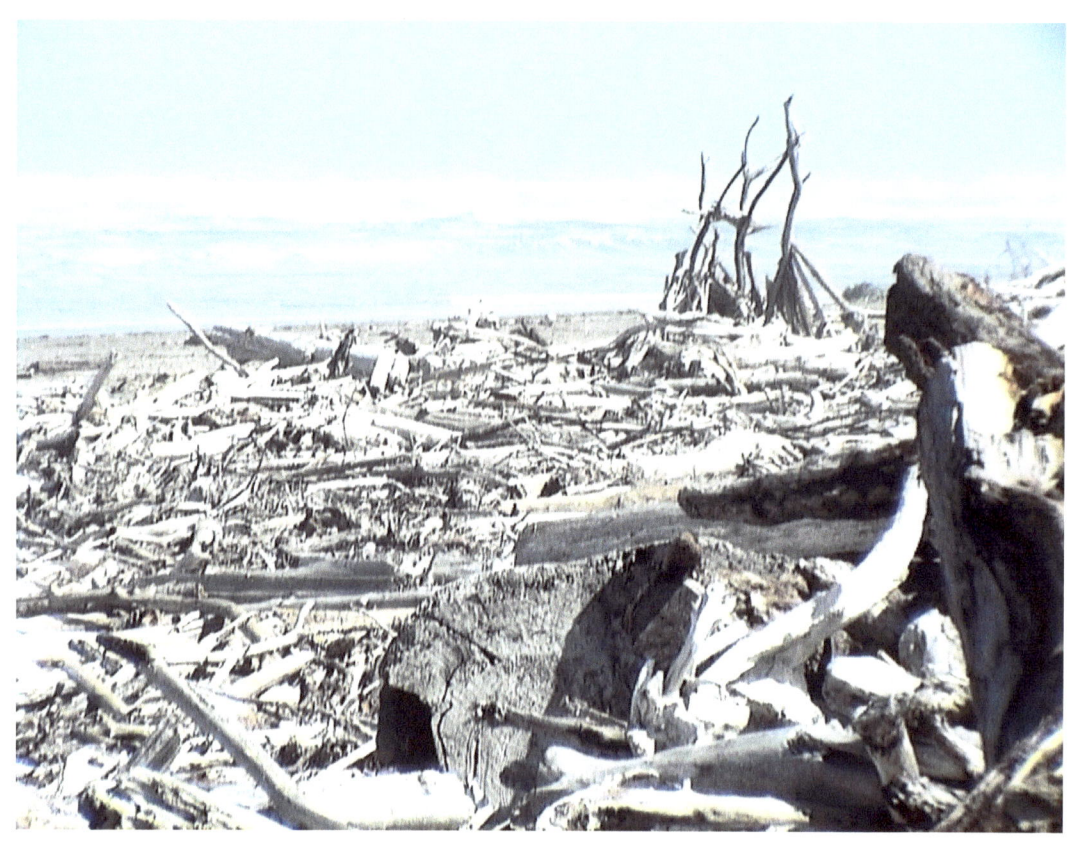

Planes of Humans

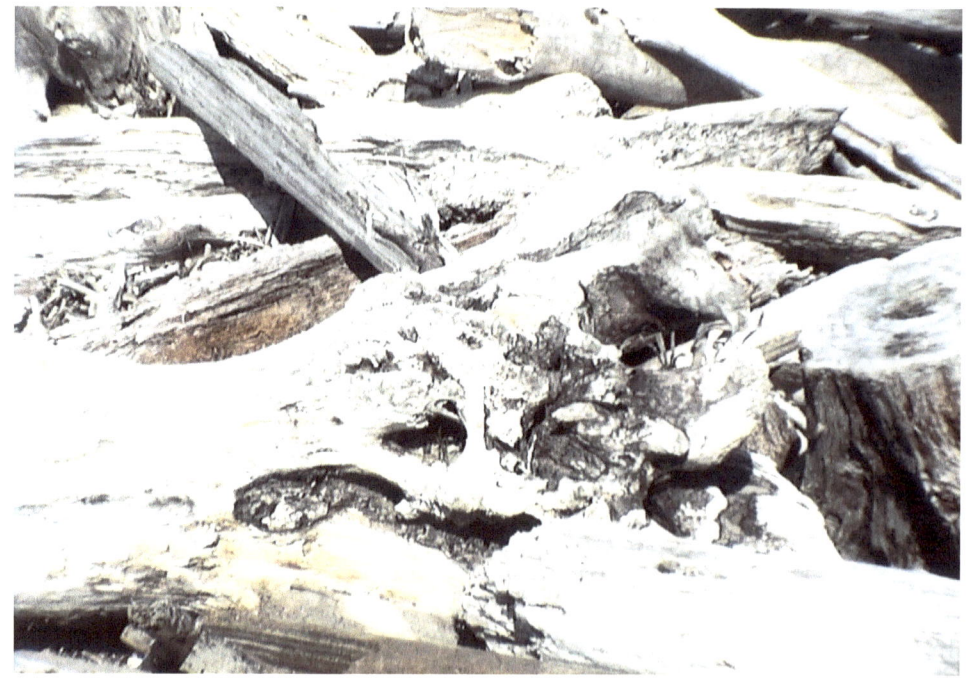

Placing Rights

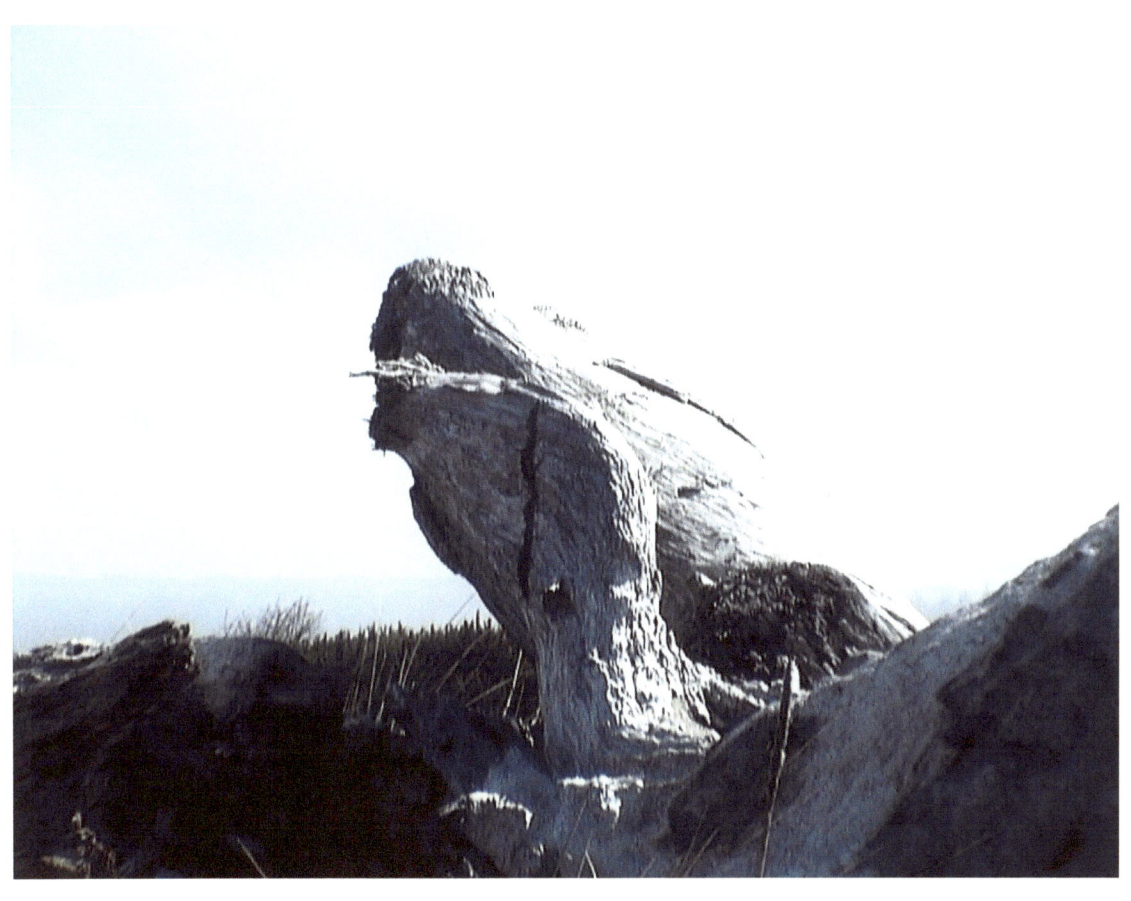

Animal log

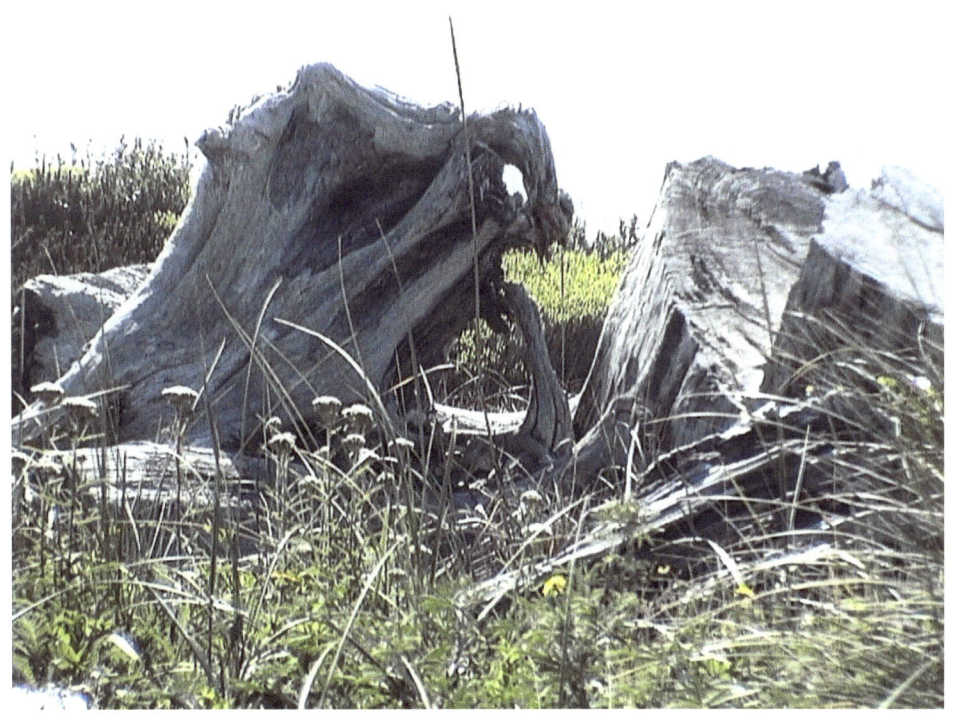

War on Estacio

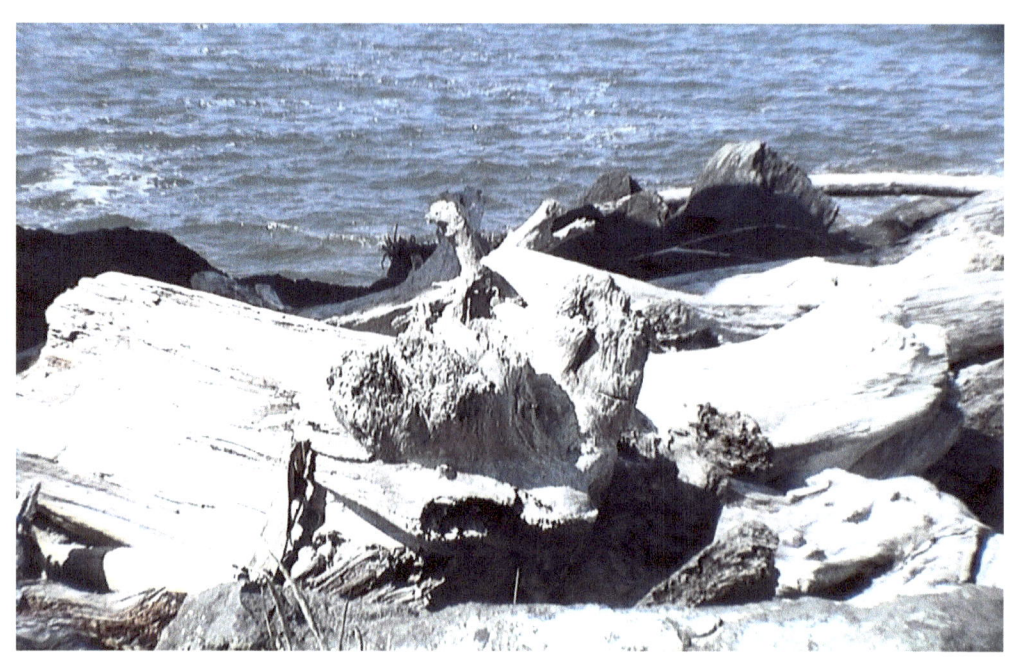

Reality of Earth

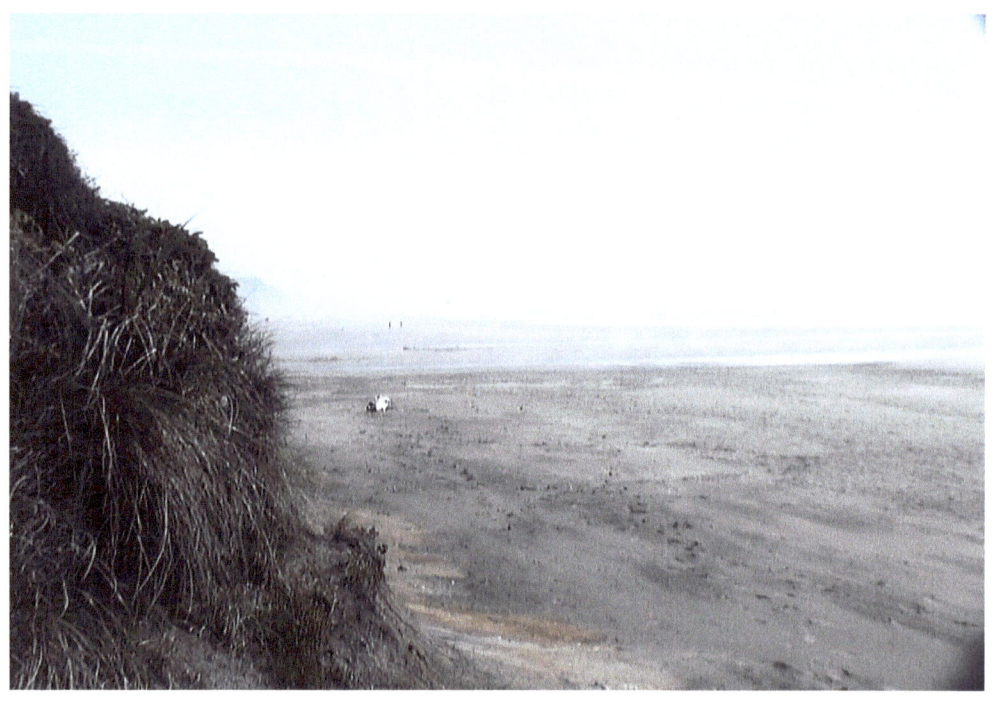

Flaps of Grey

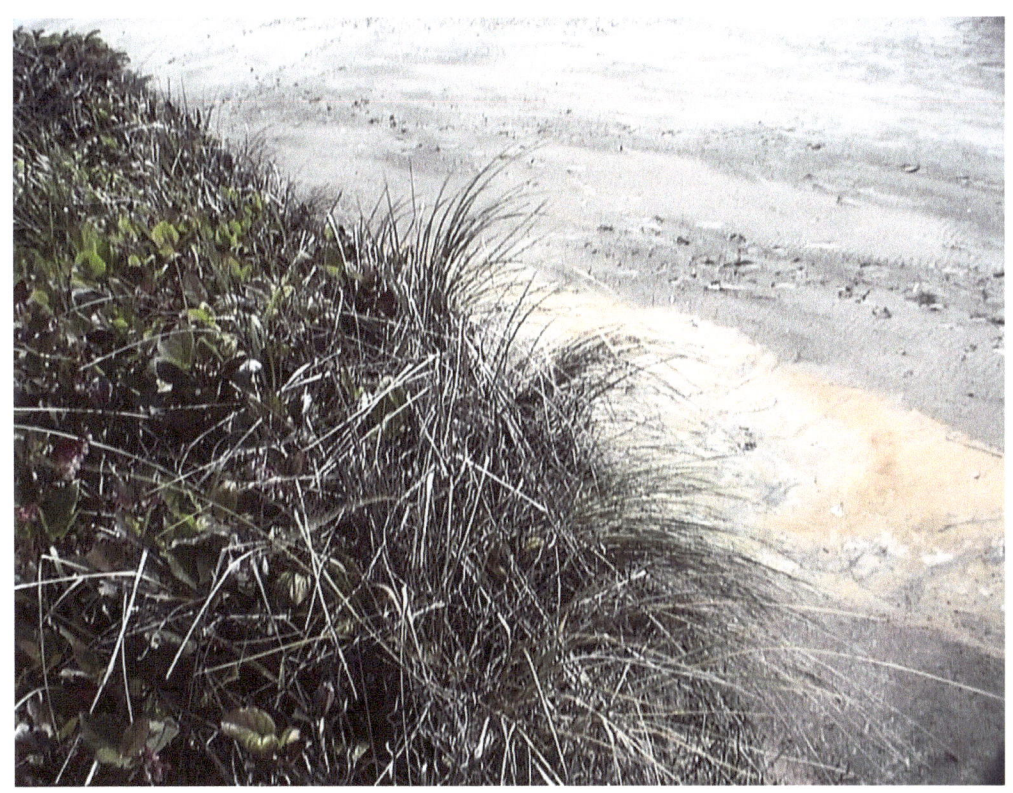

Pink Comes In

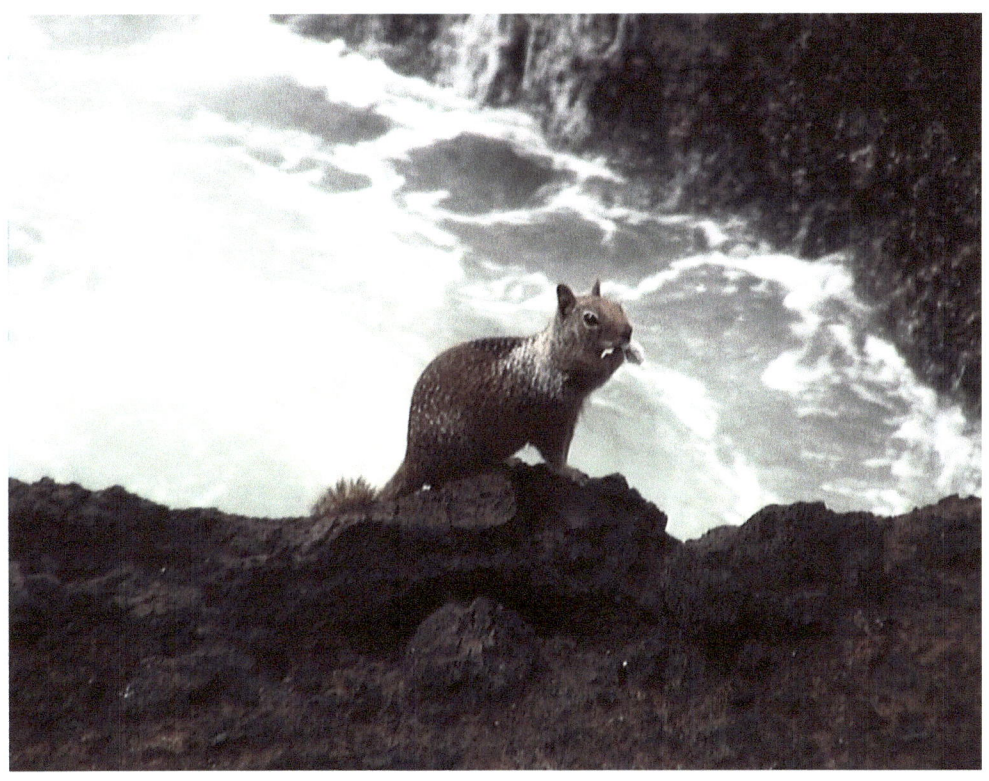

See Me

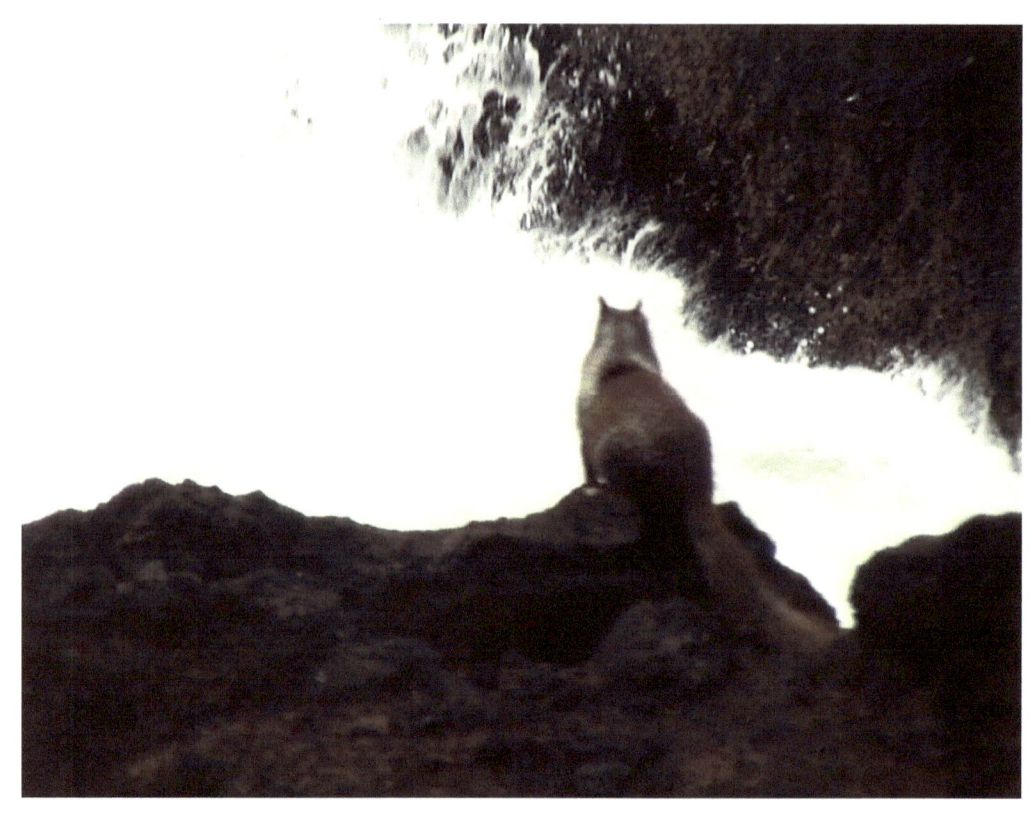

I'm Thirsty

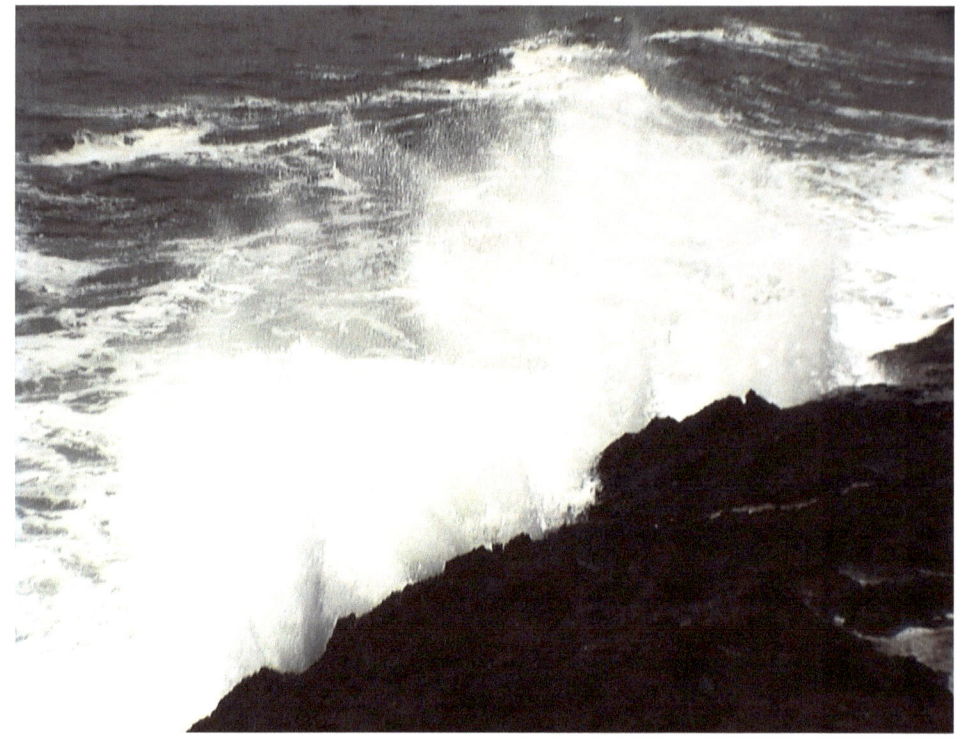

Power Flow

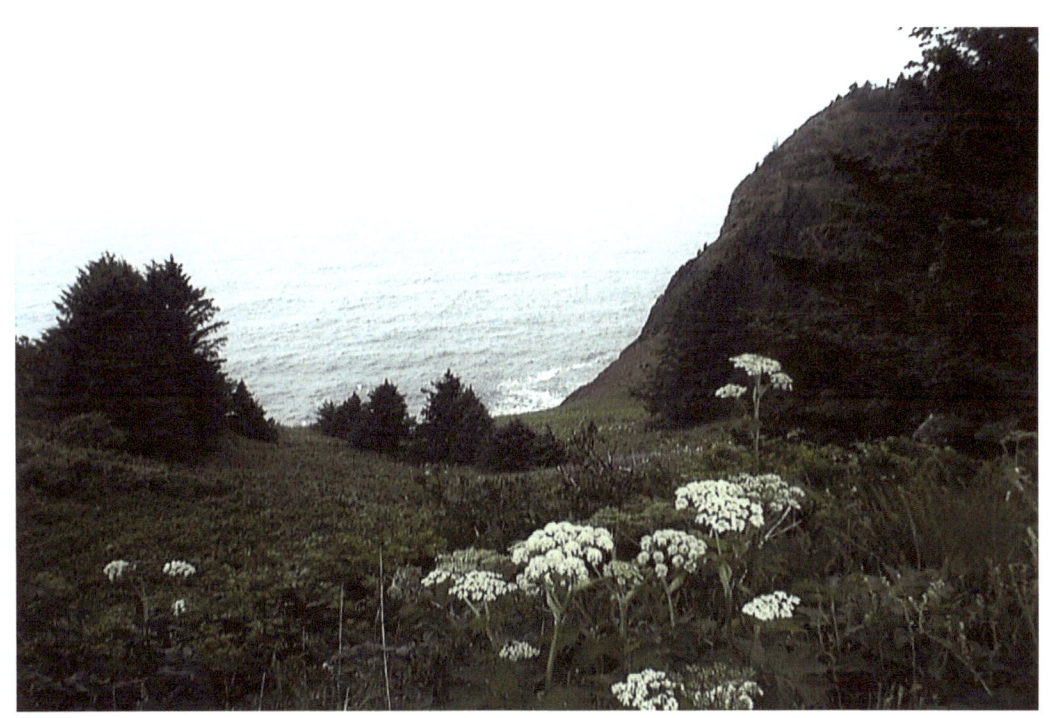

Water drops

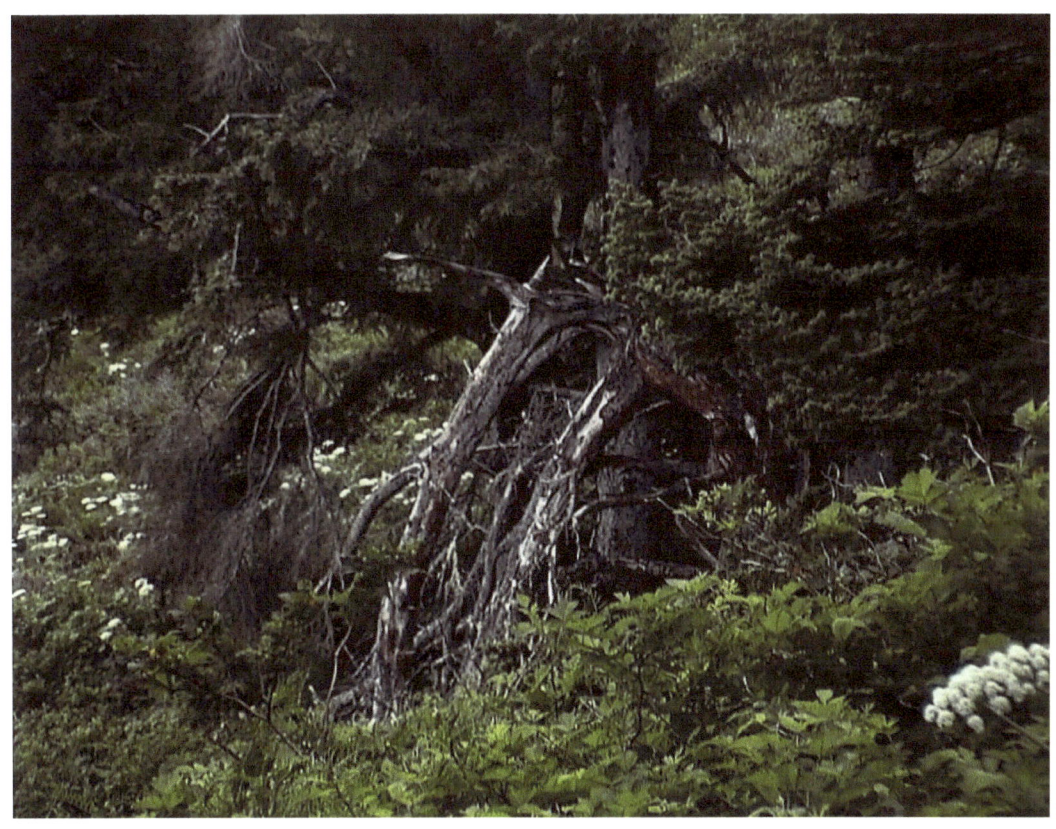

Giraffe Tree

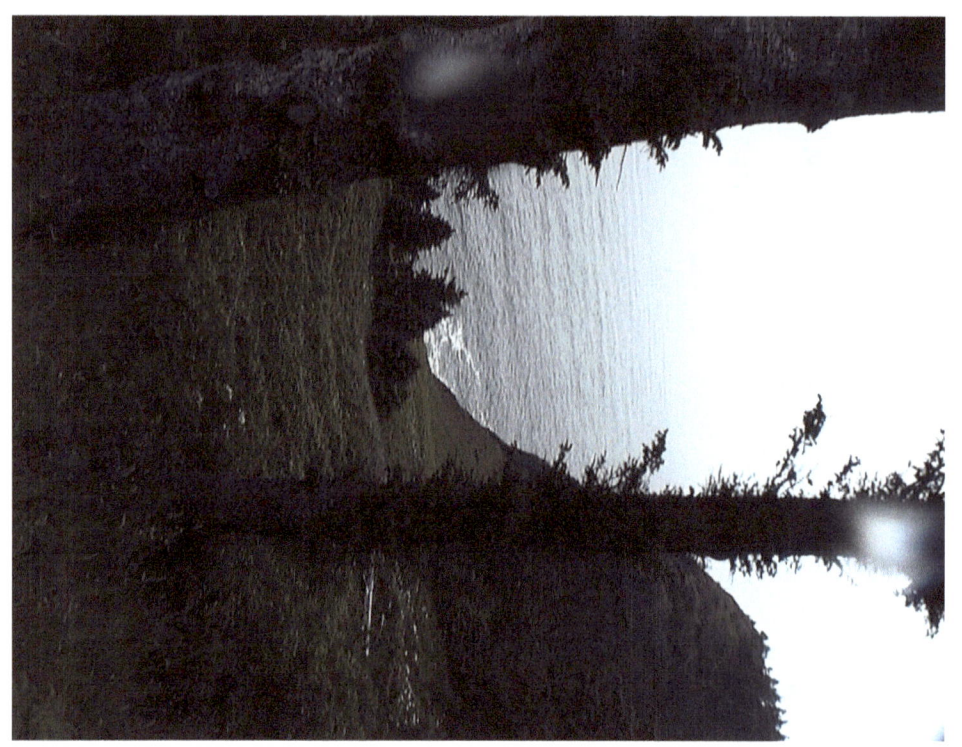

Lines of frequencies

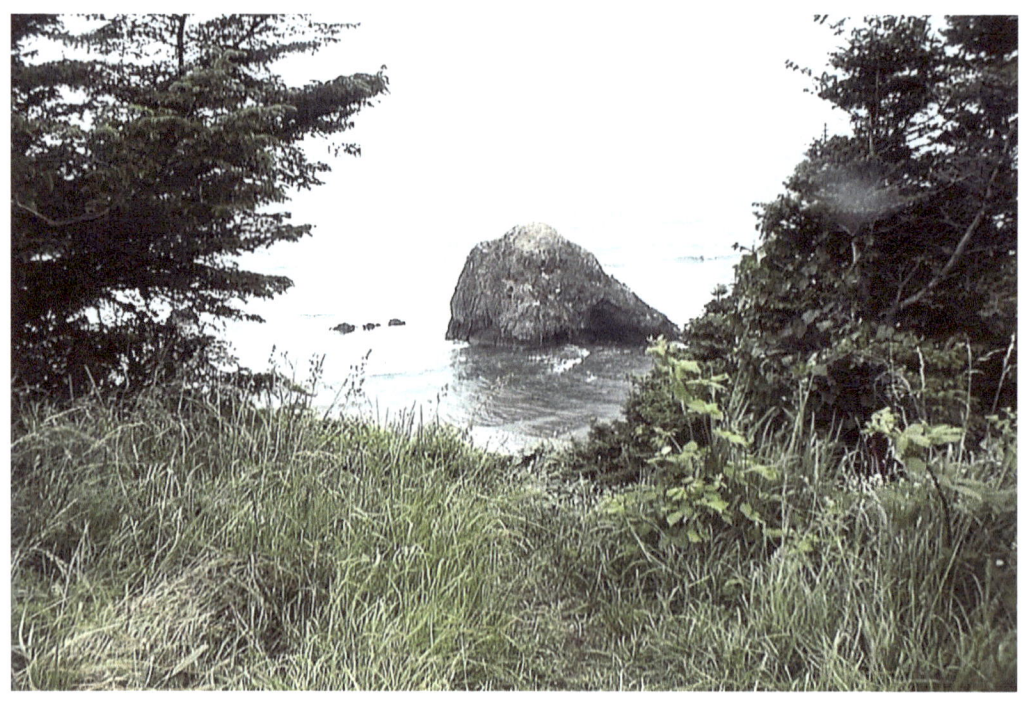

Walking to Strength

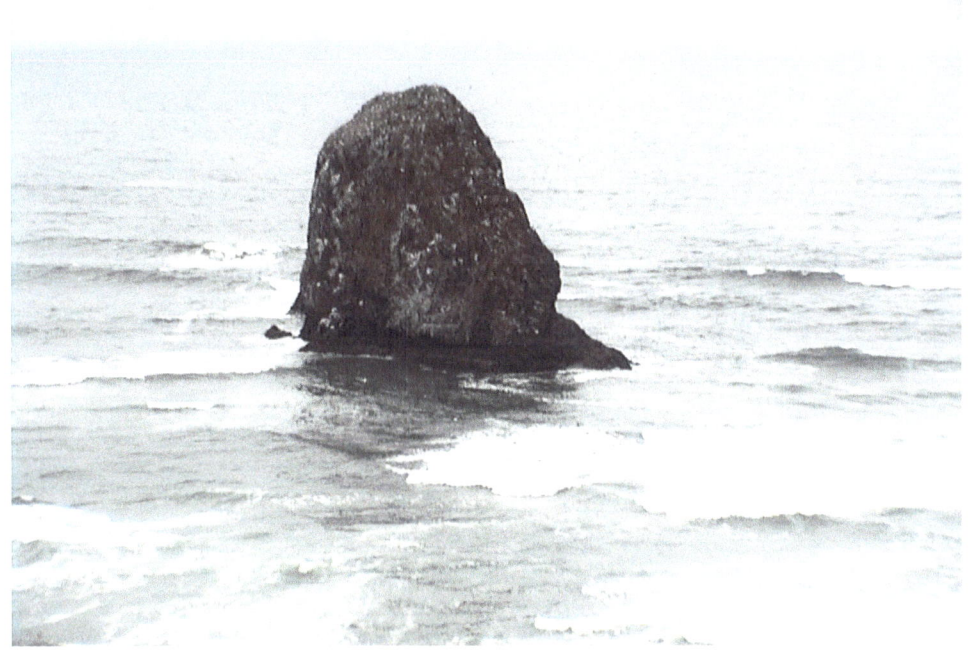

Standing in the Flow

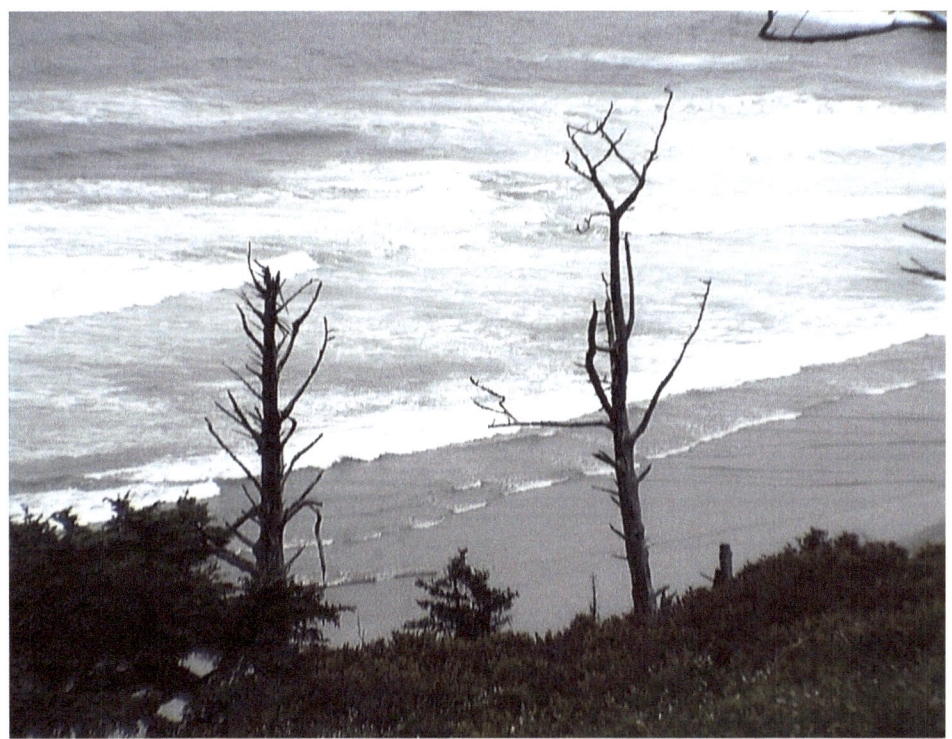

Flowing Knowledge

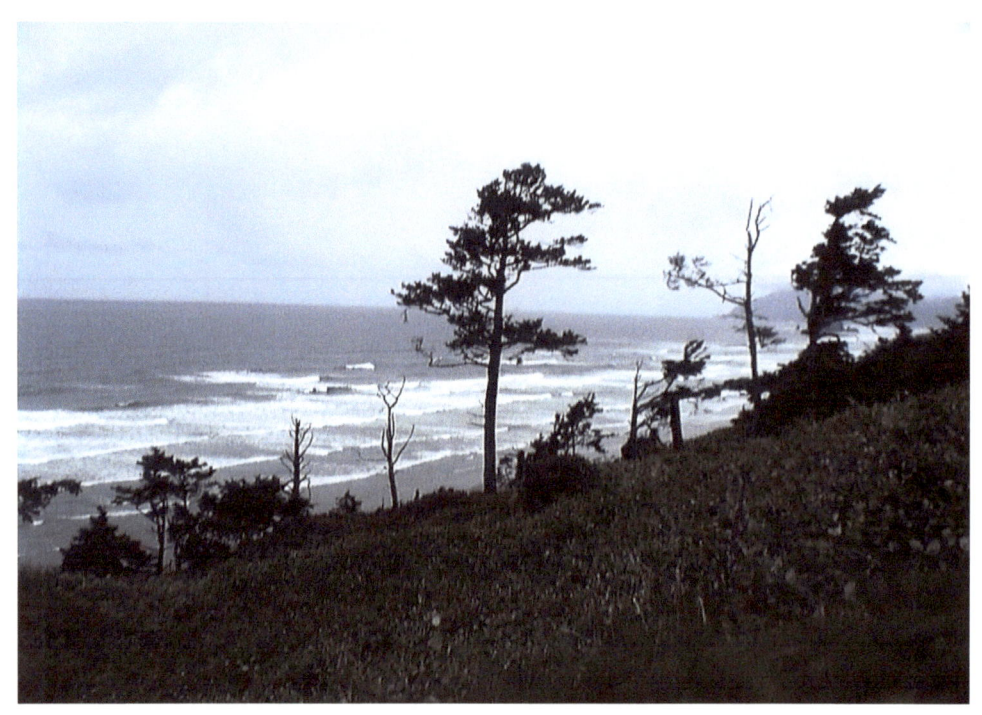

Freedom

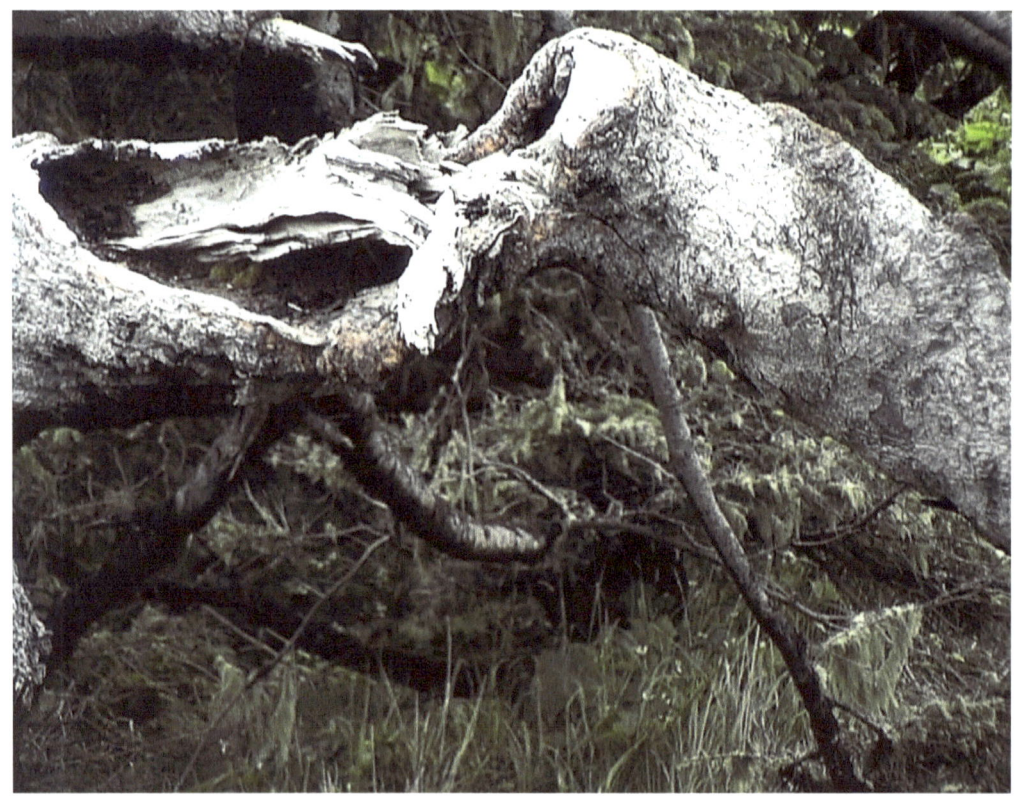

Tree Speaks

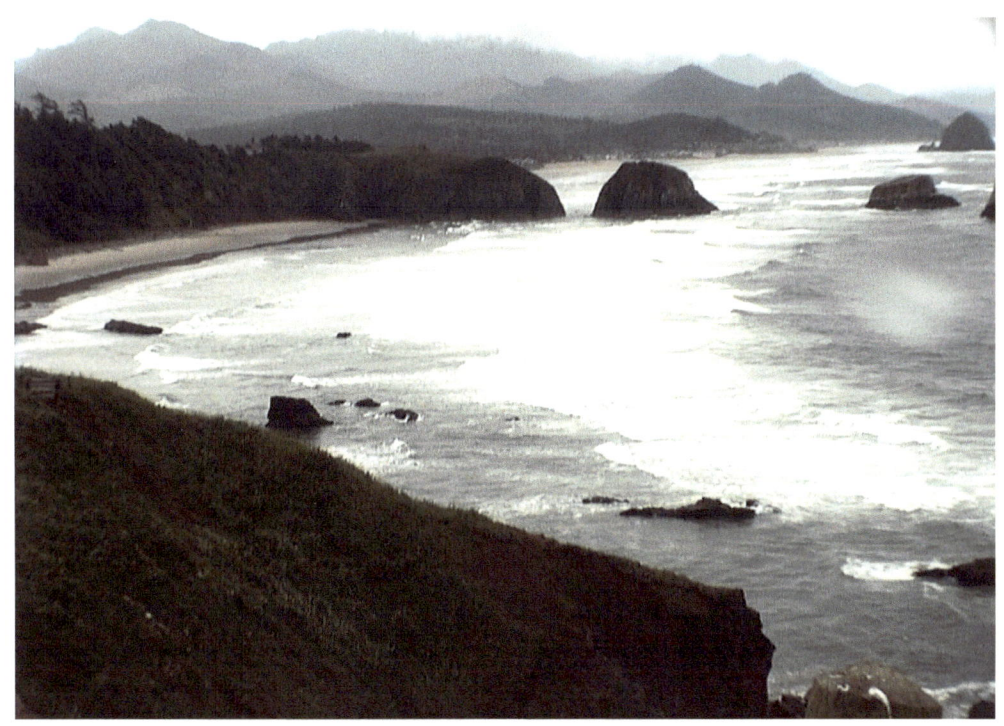

Layers of softness

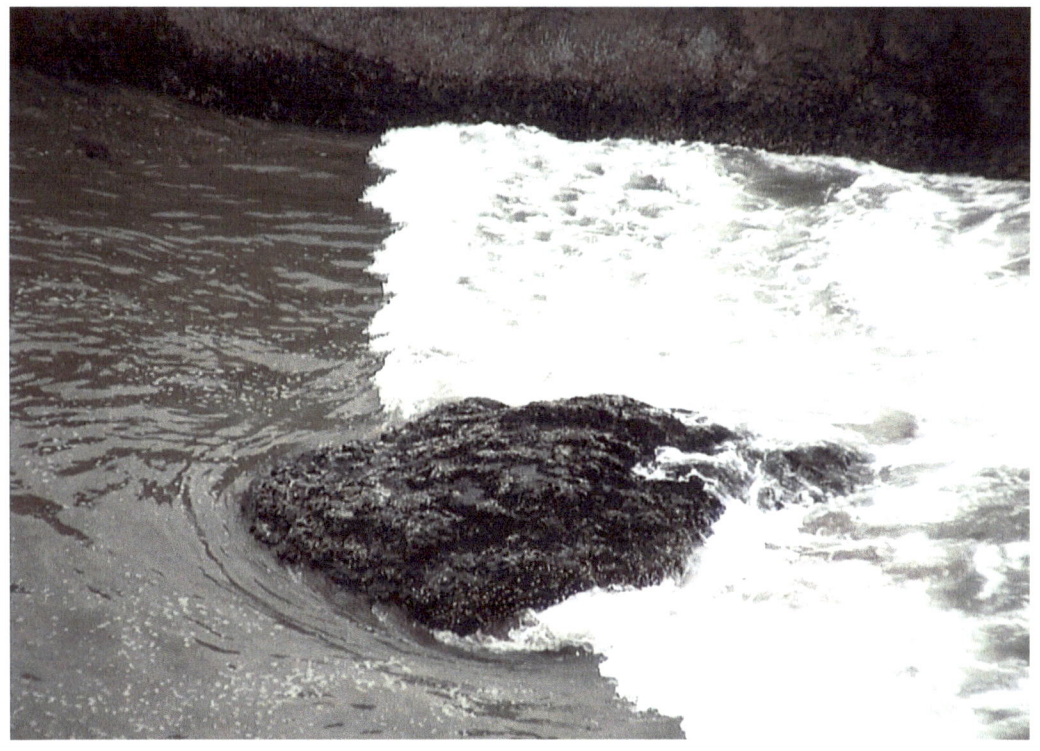

Logical Movement

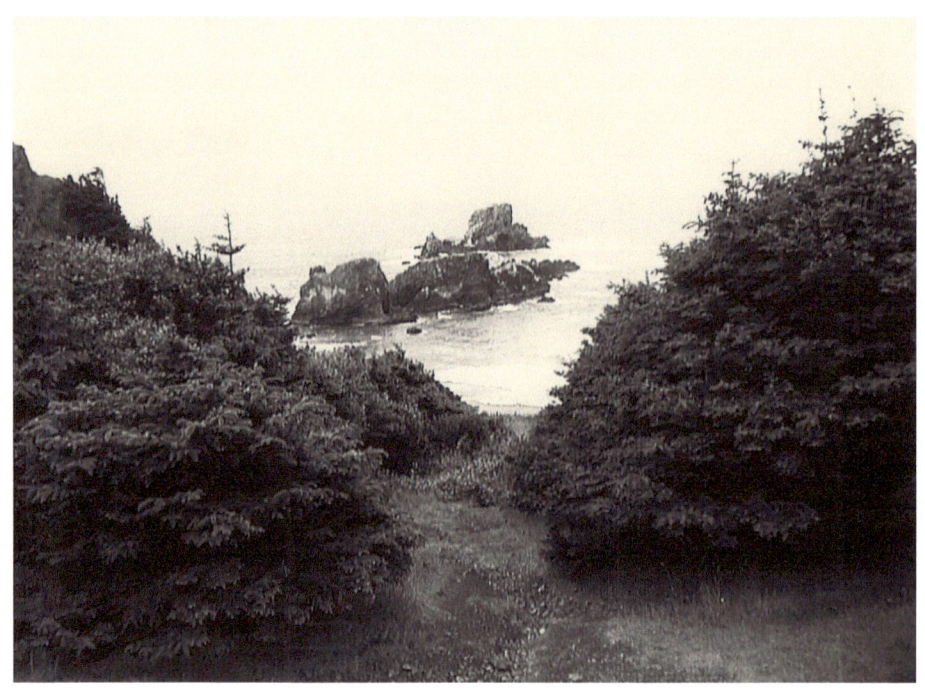

Embrace

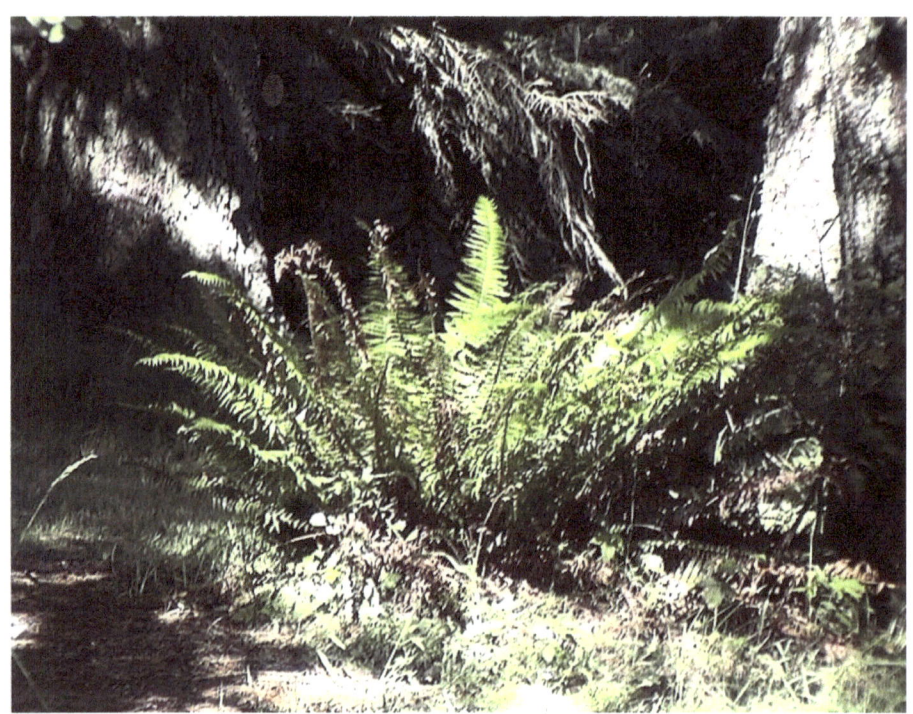

Triple Tree

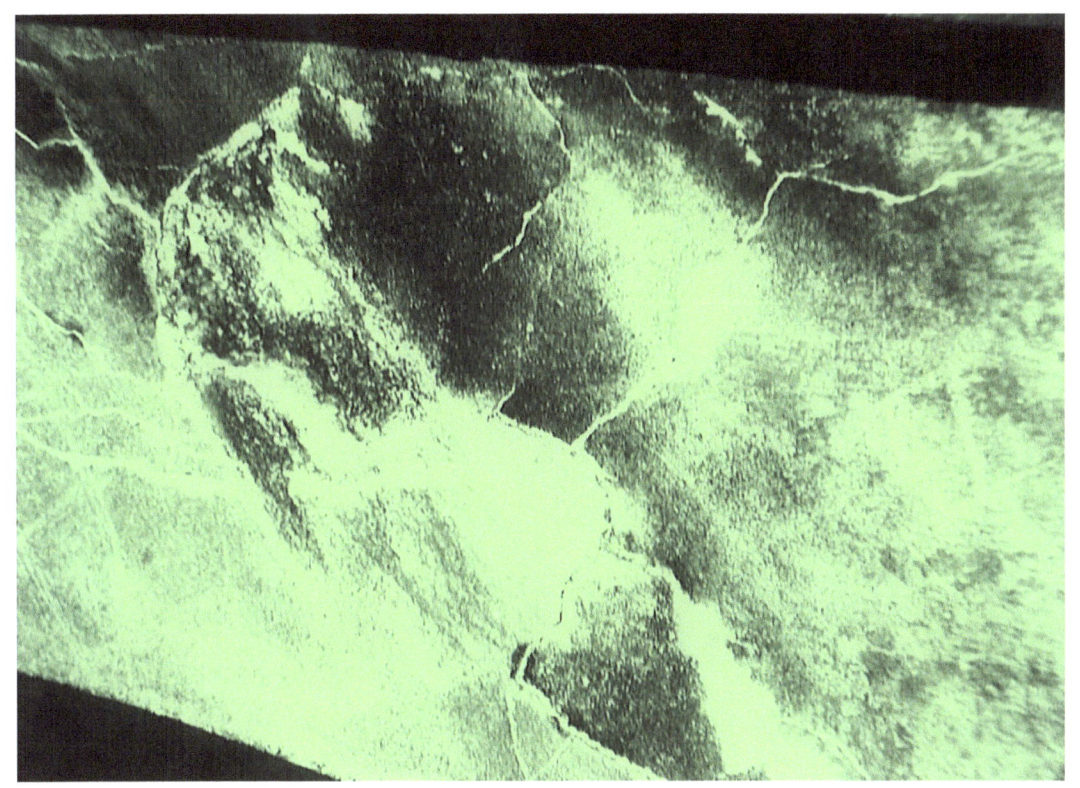
Glass Green

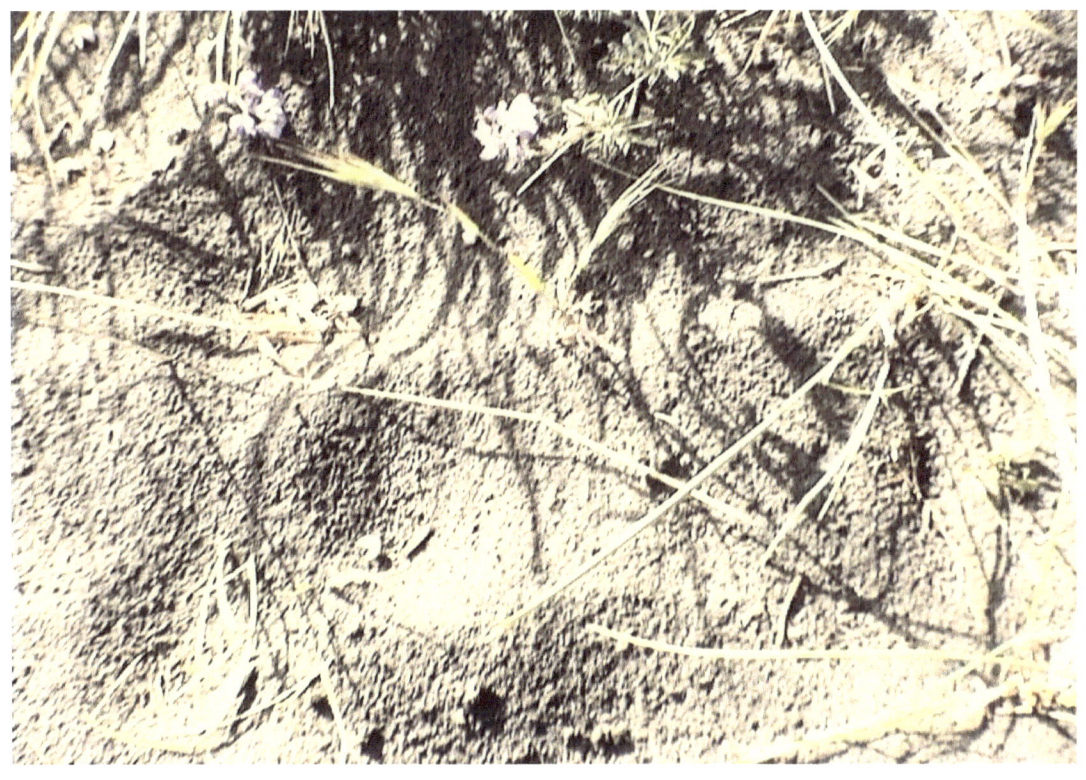
Whisper of Heart

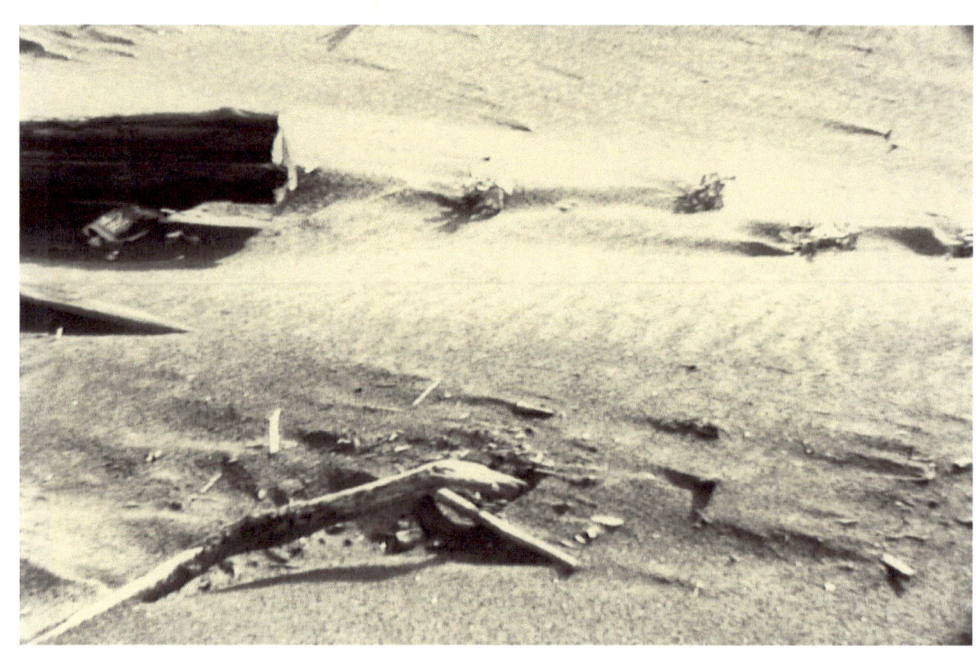

Alone

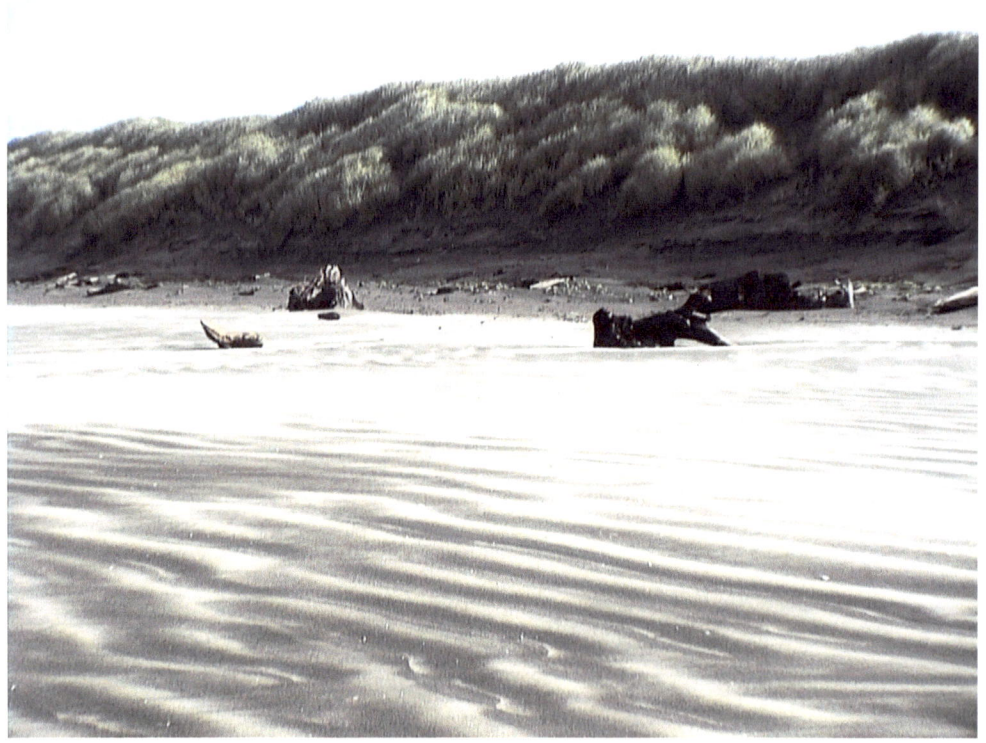

Hidden Story

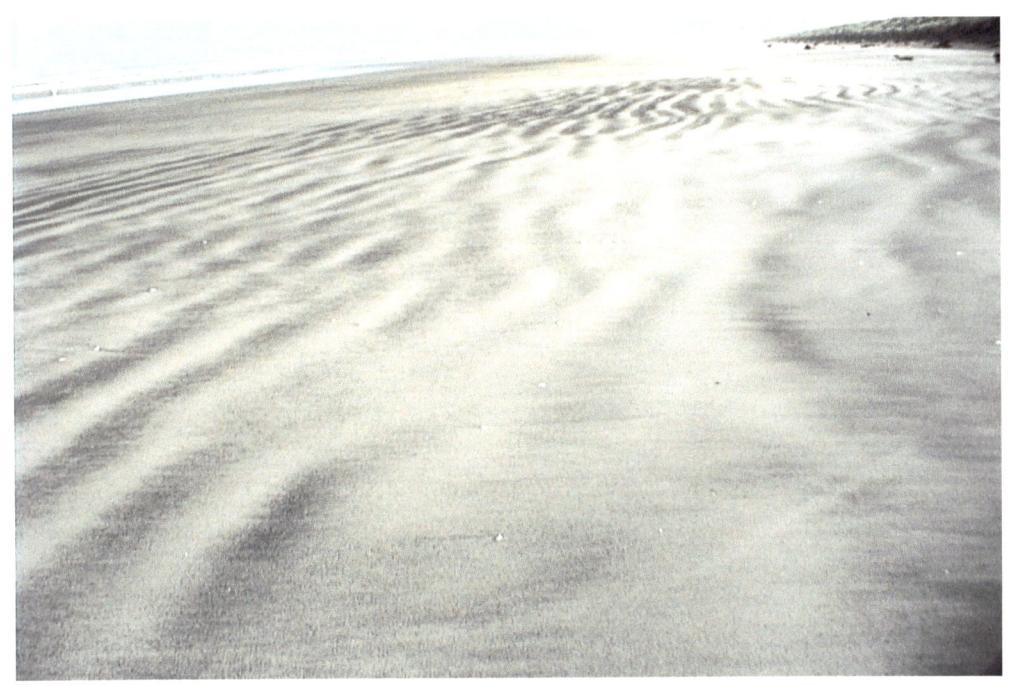

Sentimental Love flow

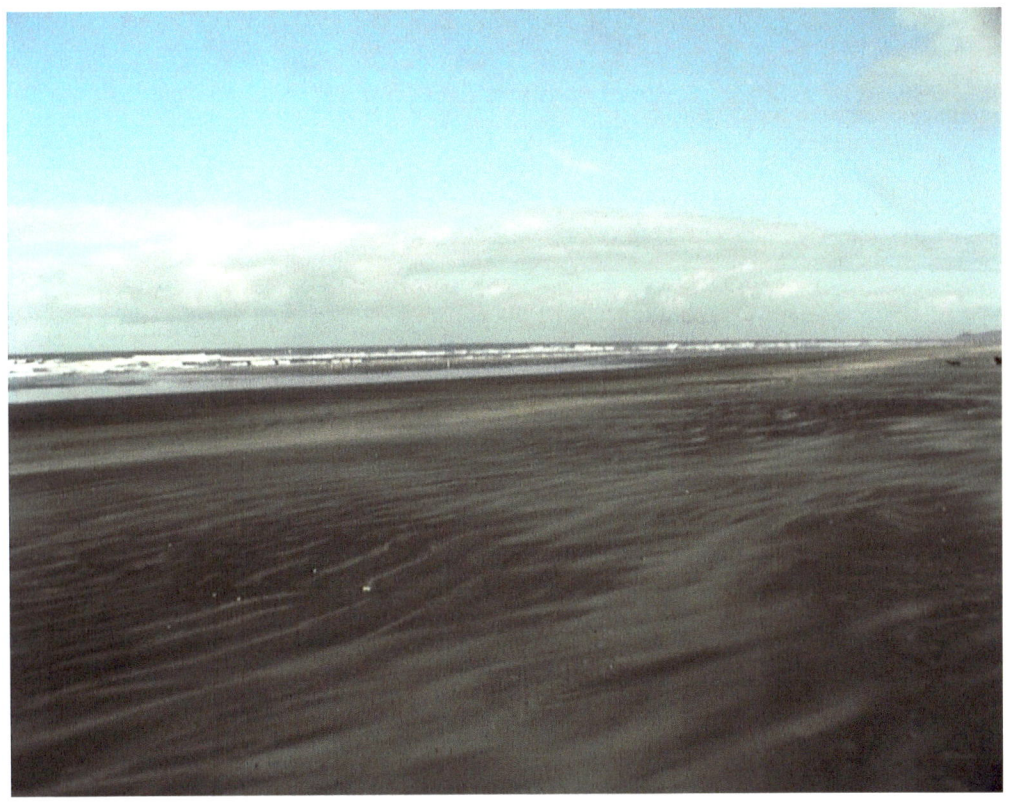

Sways of the Day

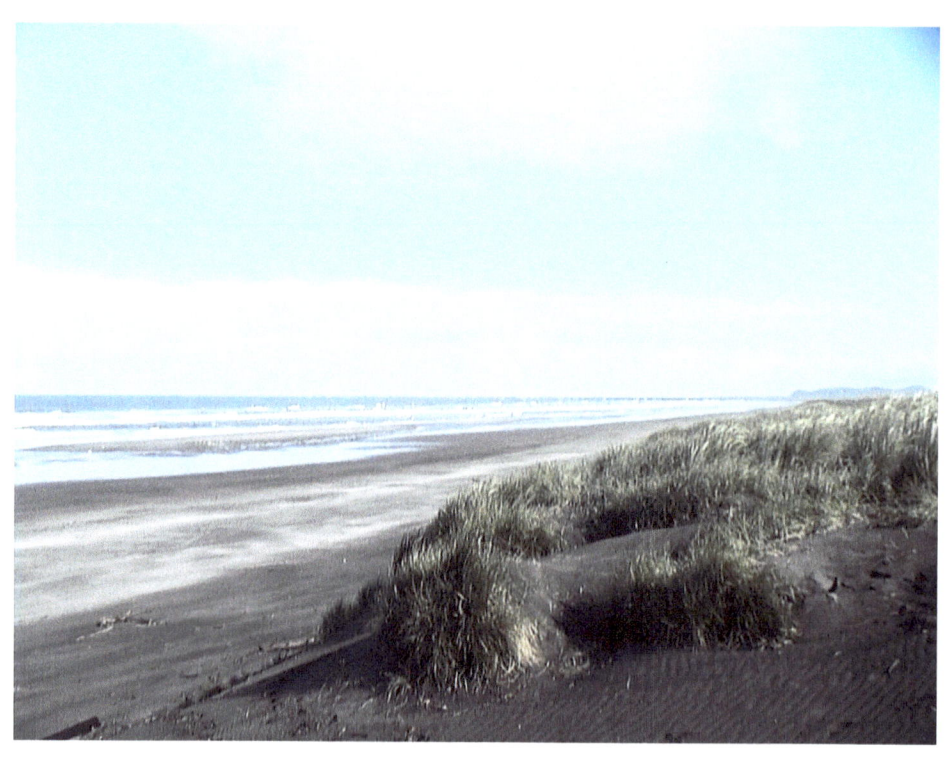

Tease of Aqua

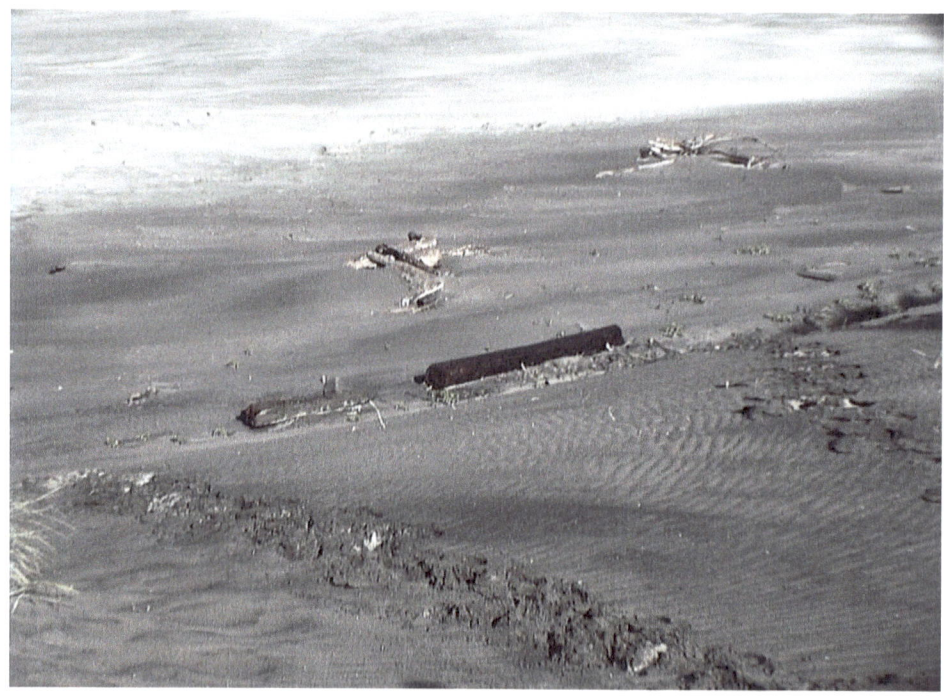

Grey Substance

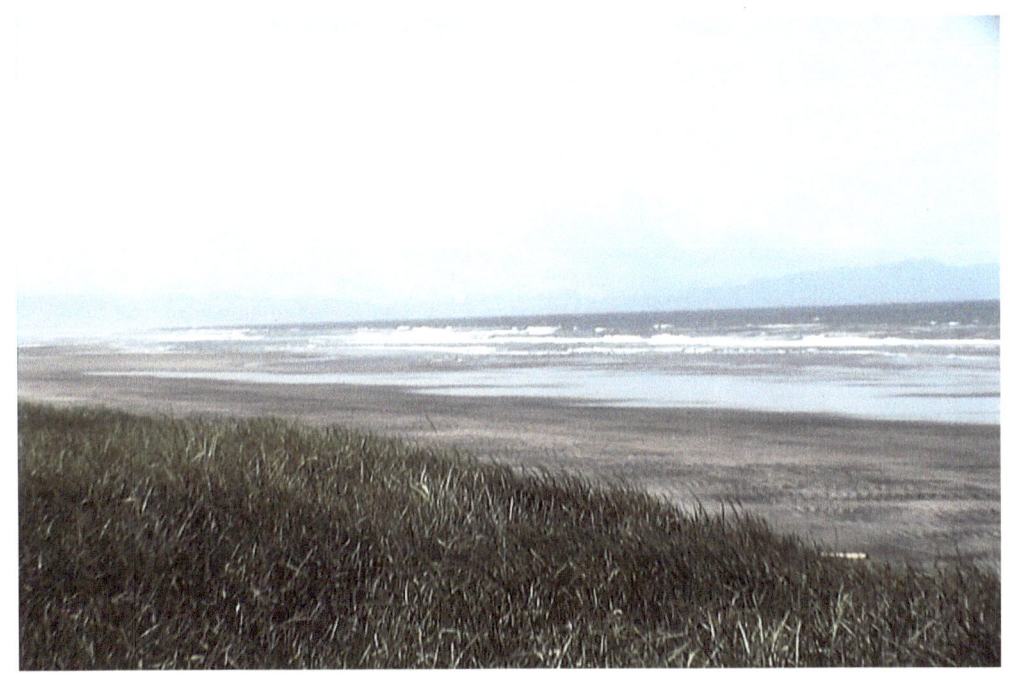

Beauty

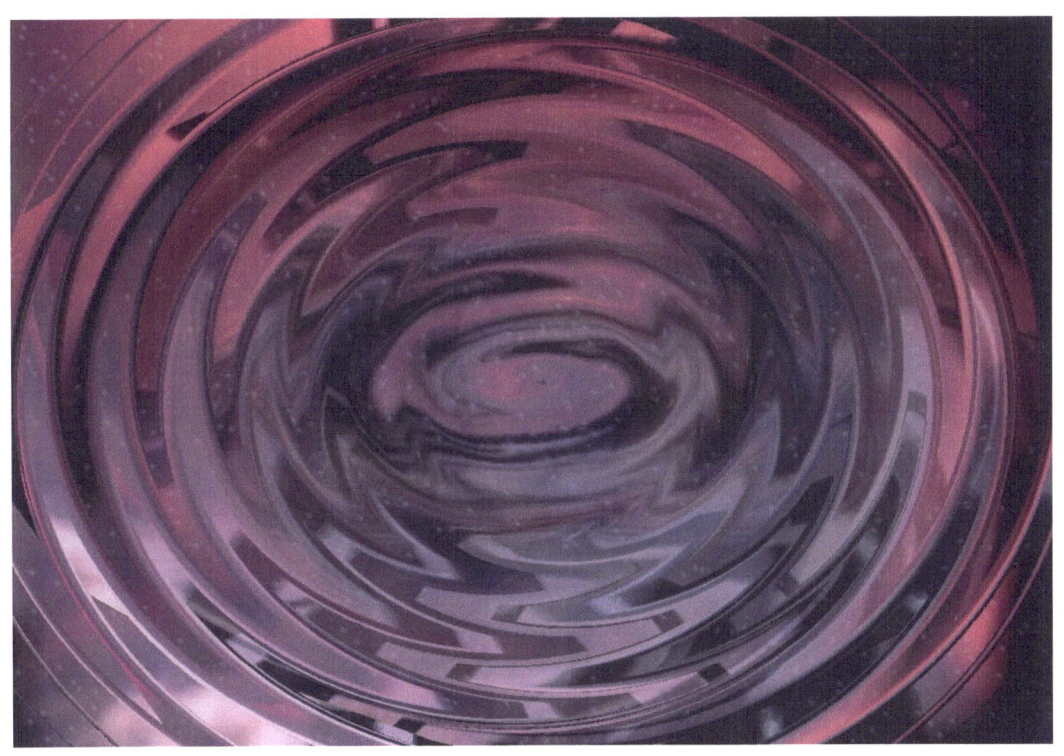

Circles of Happiness

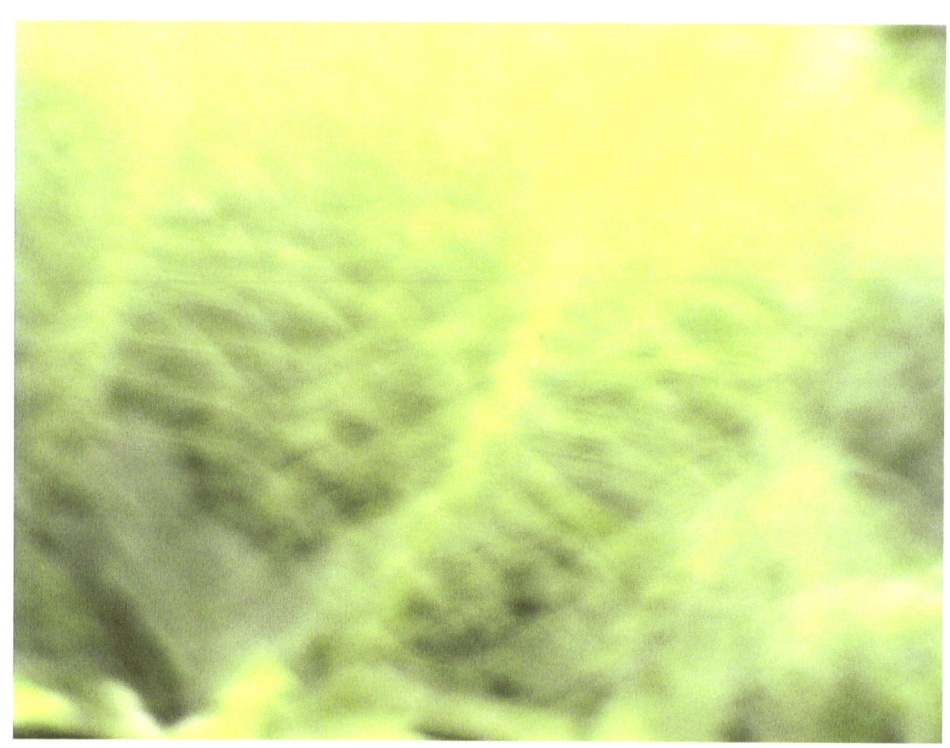

Universe Spine

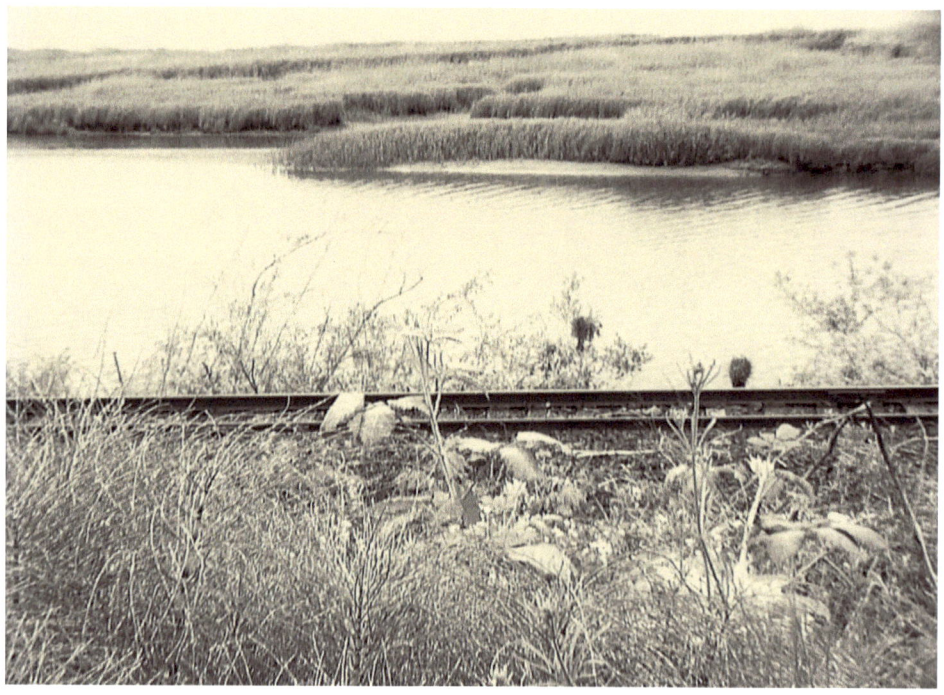

Tracks Taken

www.ingramcontent.com/pod-product-compliance
Lightning Source LLC
Chambersburg PA
CBHW040412220526
45473CB00004B/1211